8.95

THE DUTIES
OF THE
FESTIVAL SECRETARY

The Duties
of the
Festival Secretary

GEOFFREY H. NEWTON

First published in England in 1996

© 1996 Geoffrey H. Newton

Published by Ian Allan Regalia Ltd
Coombelands House, Coombelands Lane
Addlestone, Surrey, KT15 1HY
who are members of the Ian Allan Group

ISBN 0 853 18215 9

British Library Cataloguing in Publication.
A record for this book is available from the British Library.

Typeset, Printed and bound in Great Britain by
Latimer Trend & Company Ltd, Plymouth

Contents

ACKNOWLEDGEMENTS

My thanks to W.Bro. Ian Horn for the seed of an idea and Bro. Aidan Dodson for showing me the way. To my brother W.Bro. Colin Newton, W.Bro. Derek Willis and Mr. Charles Cutler, for reading drafts of the book and for the very useful comments that they made.

NOTE TO MY WIFE

My love and thanks to my wife Angela for her support throughout my masonic life.

ABOUT THE AUTHOR

Geoffrey Newton was Initiated into the Saye and Sele Lodge No. 1973, in 1976 and was Master of this Lodge in the Province of West Kent, in 1989. Prior to becoming Master of his Lodge, he spent 6 years as Festival Secretary for his Craft Lodge and for the Saye and Sele Holy Royal Arch Chapter of which he is also a member. For the last four years he has been Preceptor of the Lodge of Instruction and is now also the Secretary of his Craft Lodge. He has also served in his Lodge as Assistant Director of Ceremonies and has been promoted to the rank of Provincial Grand Steward in the Province of West Kent.

He is also a member of the West Kent Provincial Grand Stewards Lodge, the Saye and Sele Mark Lodge and the North Kent Masters Lodge.

Geoffrey Newton is a Chartered Mechanical Engineer in his business life and earlier in his career he spent five years as a technical author.

He lives in Kent and is married with a grown up family.

The Duties of the Festival Secretary

Introduction

For six years, I carried out the duties of Festival Secretary for my craft lodge and for Holy Royal Arch. During this time, the bulk of the arrangements were made by myself, with an input from another brother who helped on financial matters. This had the advantage that I was able to gain experience from the first function and then build on this experience as I went on. Having now ended my period as Festival Secretary, I continue to be approached by brethren who want to learn from my experiences. That has led to my writing this book, which is intended to be used as a step by step guide to arranging Ladies' Festivals. The procedure is taken in chronological order, from the inception through to the statement of accounts. I am conscious that some lodges choose to not have a Ladies' Festival and run a less formal dinner to mark the occasion. I suggest that the procedure which has to be followed in this instance is very similar and this book can still be used as a guide, by discounting the items that do not apply.

The whole process of arranging Ladies' Festivals lends itself to a systematic approach and there should, therefore, be no need to keep re-inventing the wheel for each function, or endure the nuisance of re-introducing the same old problems and errors into your arrangements.

Being very methodical, I had, by the end of my term as Festival Secretary, produced a range of simple formats or checklists which enabled me, with very little effort, to plan the next function, confident that all matters of importance would be addressed. Generally, the brethren who attend Ladies' Festivals, often for many years, never appreciate the amount of painstaking detail that is involved in the task. The whole process consists of often mundane but important matters, where failure in any link in the chain can cause major embarrassment on the evening. This can result, for example through a misunderstanding in not having a band or toastmaster on the night of the function. Every effort has been made to include as many examples as possible of practical problems together with their solutions.

There are an ever increasing number of pitfalls into which the unsuspecting Festival Secretary or Festival Committee can fall. Many venues and bands, for example, require contracts to be signed and, if great care is not taken at this stage, the consequence of errors can be considerable. Often there is a sliding-scale for cancellation charges for say a venue or band, which increase with time and this can make it virtually impossible to cancel the function.

It is very easy for the Festival Secretary to become complacent, especially when he has gained some experience, and you must not forget that the Master will have worked for 10 to 12 years to reach the chair and he deserves the best Ladies' Festival that you can give him. The difficulty is in arranging it often within tight financial constraints. The Master's lady will not normally have taken a high profile in his run up to the chair but she will no doubt have assisted and supported him in his masonic career, so she should be encouraged to make a useful contribution to the planning of the function.

Beware the problems arising from oneupmanship. I have seen many lodges where the functions get progressively more lavish, presumably to impress, until only the wealthiest of brethren can afford to achieve this standard. I suggest that this approach is to be discouraged as it could be a contributing factor to any given lodge not running a Ladies' Festival in the year. Never forget that another brother is going to follow and may not be able to afford to top up the cost of the function from his own pocket. Try to aim for a good average standard of function for your lodge and as a principle, run your functions to costs that will be covered by the ticket price.

Ladies' Festivals fall into three categories. Firstly, local functions which are normally within the catchment area of the lodge. These functions normally involve a great deal of work because the venue only provides the basic resources for the function, such as the hall, tables, chairs, place settings and of course staff to prepare and serve the meal. In this instance, all other items have to be arranged or be co-ordinated by the Festival Secretary. The second category is the weekend-away which includes a Ladies' Festival banquet. It is similar to the local function, but includes also the need for hotel rooms to be booked. These additional arrangements have to be superimposed on those for the banquet and this type of function is likely to be the most complex that you will have to arrange. The third category is the weekend package. This arrangement, although identical to the function previously described, is likely to be the easiest for the Festival Secretary to arrange. The hotel, or often an agent, will specify a weekend package at a given price, and you then, on behalf of the Master accept or reject the package. It is not possible to deal with every detailed combination of these three categories, so every effort has been made to highlight important differences, so that you can apply my comments to your specific requirements or arrangements.

You will note that at times it is necessary to give a guide to the likely cost of an item and as the passing of time would soon render specific costs useless, the costs have been expressed as a percentage of a typical local function ticket price.

Never forget, that the Festival Committee is in a position of trust and must be conscious of the principles of financial accountability. You will be dealing with other peoples money and fair and honest dealing must be done, and also be seen to be done. It is for this reason that our Festival Treasurer opened a separate bank account when we started organising these functions, to separate clearly the financial arrangements. With ever-increasing bank charges, it is best to explore the various methods of managing the finances.

Ladies' Festivals are traditionally considered to be non-masonic functions as they are held outside the confines of the lodge and the Master was expected to bear any losses that occurred for his Ladies' Festival. In practice, the situation is not so clear. Arrangements for the Ladies' Festivals are becoming more complicated and now carry considerable financial responsibility, with attendant legal implications. It is suggested that the ultimate responsibility for the function, will vary considerably with the agreement made between the Master and his Festival Committee. Supposing for example that the matter of financial liability has not even been broached with the Master and the Festival Secretary has set in place agreements where he has signed a contract 'for XYZ Lodge'. I believe that in this situation it would be difficult for the lodge to wash its hands of the problem. You must therefore set a very clear demarkation line between the financial responsibility of the Master for whom you are arranging the function, the lodge and the individual attendees. This example is not given to frighten a potential Festival Secretary, but it should provide a spur to ensure that he does his best to get it right. There is no substitute for experience and there is a great deal of merit in understudying the previous Festival Secretary, for a few functions, before taking over the job.

The Master of the lodge and his lady become President and Madam President for the evening of their Ladies' Festival. They are referred to as the President and his Lady, in the rest of the book, unless reference is made to instances where the Master would be making a decision in his capacity as Master of the lodge, rather than as President of his Ladies' Festival. You will note that I make frequent reference to the lodge. This has been done purely because it is not possible to make reference to all of the names applicable to the wide range of other degrees that may hold Ladies' Festivals, or arranges formal dinners for their members. The word lodge should sit easily with most readers.

As you read on, you will note that there are no checklists shown in the body of this book. The approach that has been used is to explain the procedure for arranging Ladies' Festivals in the main text by referring to the Appendices at the back of the book. I believe that as the experience of the Festival Secretary grows, there will be a greater tendency to just refer to the Appendices and it will be easier to locate them in one place at the back of the book and not have to search through the text for them.

Approach to the task

Considering the composition of the Festival Committee. In practice, the composition of the Festival Committee varies considerably with what can be called normal practice. I have no intention of making a categoric statement on what is right or wrong, but to give the advantages and disadvantages and to express what I know, has consistently been successful. Some lodges employ a formal committee which can consist of up to six lodge members. I have found that making detailed arrangements often necessitates the Festival Secretary having to react to problems or situations quickly and I suggest that having to get a committee together on a regular basis and then find that only a few of the committee do any work, fills me with horror. I believe that apart from the logistic difficulties involved, there is an increased problem of reaching a consensus in decision making, together with an increased risk that an important matter will simply drop through the cracks. Through the whole of my time as Festival Secretary, I took the lead in all detailed arrangements and was supported by a Festival Treasurer, who happened to be my own brother (W.Bro. Colin Newton). This approach worked well and had the advantage that the detailed arrangements fell naturally into my territory, whilst the Festival Treasurer kept a close eye on financial matters. It is clearly not necessary for the Treasurer to be a financial wizard, but it does help a great deal if he has some experience of dealing with matters of finance, or is at least logical of thought and is a good administrator.

Arrangements for Ladies' Festivals can be started 12-18 months before the function date. In my case, both craft and chapter functions could be running, so it was common for at least two functions to be at various stages of planning, at the same time. It cannot be stressed too highly that all aspects of the arrangements should be dealt with promptly and methodically, as I have found that it is easy enough for problems to occur, without asking for them. The most simple and practical way of keeping control, is to open a separate file or folder for each function that you run, so that all relevant information is kept together and in date sequence. It is suggested that a file in which each paper is entered onto a tag, which is affixed to the top of the file and all papers threaded onto it, has the advantage that papers will automatically remain in chronological order. I find that the wallet type folders, in which papers are just slipped in, has the disadvantage that it is all too easy to get them out of order, but this must be your choice.

There should be no mystique surrounding the arrangement of Ladies' Festivals. There are a large number of detailed arrangements which have to be made and in practice they vary little from function to function. Many Festival Secretaries start their planning for each function and deal with matters as if it was their first, by referring to the file for the last function that they arranged and use it as a rough guide for the sequence of events. I can see no merit in relying on memory and therefore forgetting important features or introducing different errors every time. Remember, that if you have followed a methodical approach, then the maxim, 'if you have arranged one, you can arrange them all', does apply. By the time that I had completed my time as a Festival Secretary, I had developed the main Ladies' Festival checklist, at Appendix 1. You will note that the items on the main checklist are not in chronological order, as this would enormously increase its size and would involve numerous duplications of items and in any case, flexibility is required to take into account the variation in requirements for each function. I suggest that you use my checklist as a start point and when you have read this book, you can then develop the list to suit your own purpose. This checklist proved to be invaluable and was always the first piece of information that went into my file. You will find that if you are able to put the checklist onto a word processor, it will help if you leave a few lines of space between each item, so that you can add handwritten notes when you make the detailed arrangements. As you progress through the various stages you will find that you will continually refer back to this list when checking on progress.

Preparation for the Meeting with the President and his Lady

In theory, the President and his Lady are free to decide every detail of the requirements for their function, but in reality this is not very practical. You will find that if every detail is decided by committee, even if that committee only consists of the President, his lady and yourself, it would take up an excessive amount of time, with you continually arranging progress meetings to control arrangements.

I have always tried to strike a balance, whereby the President and his Lady have reasonable choice on the major items that contribute to their evening, but I also take into account the practicality of having to make sensible progress in the arrangements. The major items that, I would suggest, require a significant input from the President and his Lady are, function date, venue, band, singer or cabaret, ladies present, menu cards and the meal for the function. If you have not carried out the duties of Festival Secretary before and you do not want to appear to be a new boy, you will need to carry out some initial planning. The object of this exercise is for you to obtain sufficient information to give the President and his Lady a range of options for each of these items. Bear in mind that if the President has not been involved in the duties of a Festival Secretary, he will not necessarily have a full appreciation of what is involved. The following notes should cover the majority of situations and these are taken in turn:

Function Date

It may at first seem unnecessary to consider a function date before you have discussed the matter with the President and his Lady. This is not so, as the time of year and therefore the weather can play an important part in your arrangements. I recall that we had arranged a weekend-away Ladies' Festival about 70 miles from our home base, on the 1st of March. On the main day of travel for the guests, we had a very heavy snow fall, which caused travelling problems. The consequences of 50 per cent of the guests not being able to even get to the function and the attendant legal wrangle with the hotel can be imagined. We were very lucky on that occasion as a very rapid thaw followed which saved the day. Your own lodge may have a pattern whereby you always arrange a function date at a set time in the year, bearing in mind that the function ought to be arranged when the President is actually in the chair. We had one instance where this was not possible and it was overcome by the Master clearing this date with the Master Elect, as it fell into his year. If there are no other pre-conditions, I use a simple formula. Local functions can be arranged for any time in the year, but for weekends-away, I now exclude the winter months, such as December to March inclusive. For a number of years we have arranged weekend-away functions in late September. This month normally puts charges outside the high-season charge band and we have consistently been very lucky and have enjoyed marvellous weather. It is suggested that you be prepared to discuss these aspects with the President and his Lady. If the President should apply pressure to opt for a risky winter weekend-away, the Festival Secretary must be very clear in his mind where the financial liability lies, if the function is likely to fail, and act accordingly. I would go as far as putting my concerns to him in writing. In my experience, discussion alone normally results in a triumph for good old common sense.

Venue

The main decision which has to be made, is whether to have a local function, or whether to have a weekend-away. The decision, which the President and his Lady have to make, is never going to satisfy everyone. The younger members of the lodge will perhaps prefer a local function, where they can arrange for baby sitters and also keep the costs down to reasonable levels and the older members will prefer the weekend-away. You need to be aware of the arrangement which suits the majority of the members and if you are not, then you should find out, because if you get it wrong, you could have problems. Your lodge may, however, have a set venue, which is used year after year. This is often the easiest option as it has the advantage that the booking with the venue just rolls on year after year and all of the arrangements will be virtually identical. In this instance you will have no excuses for getting it wrong. Your main checklist should reflect the arrangements down to the last detail, so that anyone could arrange the function. Most venues, for continuity of business, offer the lodge who used the venue at the same time the previous year, the first refusal on the next years booking. My lodge and chapter are almost totally nomadic and switch from a range of local venues and weekends-away to different hotels with no particular pattern. This policy has a major disadvantage, and understandably it is the direct reverse of the advantage to staying at one venue long term. The venues, as just mentioned, wait until the previous booking has been taken up, or refused. Thus, at most venues, the Festival Secretary is continually running into the year of the function before he has a firm booking date. As mentioned, weekend-away functions fall into two categories. The first is where the arrangements for the Ladies' Festival have to be arranged from first principles, as for a local function, with hotel bookings superimposed on the arrangements.

The second category is the weekend package, where you can obtain good value packages, off season, by many of the larger seaside hotels. The advantage of the last arrangement is that as Festival Secretary, you have very little work to do, in that an agent will make the majority of arrangements for you. The disadvantage is that you are often limited on choice, in that the band for example may be a resident band, which is not what you would want or expect. It could be assumed that in this instance you would not need the information contained in this book, but this could not be further from the truth. The acid test for these package deals is, what are you going to get for your money? Using the information in this book, you should be in a position to ask the hotel representative or agent searching questions, because all of the arrangements detailed in this book, still have to be made, irrespective of who makes them. You must therefore, after some thought, be able to offer the President and his Lady a range of options, for local venues and for weekend-aways, depending on what the normal lodge practice is. If you have no personal knowledge of the venues, ask the festival secretaries of other lodges, masonic friends, look at masonic magazines and even look in yellow pages, which are of course produced across the whole country. If you need information on hotels for weekends-away, there are many published guides which can be found in any good bookshop. I am sure that at the end of your research, you will be spoiled for choice. You will want to take your research, no further than having a feel for the general requirements, what type of function are you going to arrange, where will it be and when will it be?

Band

It is suggested, that apart from the venue, the selection of the band plays a major part in setting you on the right path for an enjoyable function. Although the President and his Lady are unlikely to have any knowledge of the availability of bands, you must get a feel for what is going to be required. This subject prompts many questions which I am not in a position to answer, so I highlight some of the main questions which need to be answered at this stage. What is the average age of the lodge members, do they want a modern band or are they a little more staid? This can be a difficult choice, in that there is often an age spread in a lodge. Remember that loud music is the meat and drink of younger members, but it can completely spoil the evening for those of mature years. This is discussed in greater depth at a later stage. Be prepared to discuss the requirements with the President and his Lady. Details of bands can be obtained from yellow pages or other sources, but this has the disadvantage that you have to rely on how good the band say that they are. Self praise is often no recommendation, so I have found that it is best to obtain details from other festival secretaries, or, if you have time, ask any band leader for his card at functions that you and your friends attend and you will soon build up an impressive list of contacts.

Singer or Cabaret

Arrangements are often made for someone to sing the 'Ladies' Song' to the President's Lady and this requirement can perhaps be met by a talented lodge member, or by hiring a professional singer. The professional singer would normally bring his own accompanist and microphone. The mid-evening cabaret is another option which has the advantage that it does provide a 'gap filler', when the band go for their break. The only counter to this is that when you consider what you are having to pay for the band, further reducing the time that they are to play makes the cabaret, in my opinion, poor value for money. Under normal circumstances, the President would be expected to pay for the singer or cabaret.

Ladies' Present

It is customary to give each lady a present at the function. Normal practice will give a guide to what you would normally spend on a present, but it will certainly feature as a significant cost in the ticket price. You might expect that attendance at Ladies' Festivals would be exactly 50 per cent men and 50 per cent ladies. I have consistently found that this is not the case, as approximately 55-60 per cent of those attending our Ladies' Festival are ladies. The attendance of members daughters or widows attending with friends always seems to push the balance over 50 per cent. There are a number of options available for buying presents. This can range from the firms advertised in masonic magazines, who provide catalogues of items which can be supplied in quantity, pre-wrapped and even on a sale or return basis. This service does have the advantage that it saves some work and does remove the risk of making a mistake with numbers attending, but it comes at a price. Many Festival Secretaries accept the burden, or ask another brother to help, by buying the presents and wrapping them yourself. When estimating the costs for this item do not forget to include the cost of packaging, which can be significant. It is certainly worth making enquiries around the lodge, to see if any brother has contacts who can help to buy suitable presents at a favourable price. Before discussing with the President and his Lady, obtain some present catalogues, because even if you don't intend to use them, they can give you some useful ideas. Also make up a list of the last five years presents, so that you don't inadvertently duplicate. Be alive to problems which can be caused by the size of the ladies present. There is often very limited space on a dining table. so keep in the back of your mind whether the size or shape of the present will fit easily on the table, or whether it will be necessary to appoint table stewards to distribute the presents.

Menu Cards

This may seem to be a minor item, but the menu card is likely to be the opportunity for a colour co-ordinated table layout at the function. In addition, the card contains a wealth of detail, the menu, those who are to propose toasts and make replies. It also mentions the name of the band and the toastmaster. See a typical menu card layout at Appendix 2. The detailed requirements of the content of the menu card are dealt with under the initial meeting with the President and his Lady. You should bear in mind that the colour of the menu card, table cloth, serviettes and candles, when considered properly, gives a very favourable impression on the night. The appearance of a well laid out and colour co-ordinated table gives a wonderful impression, so that you will be well down the road to success and the guests have not even taken their seats. If in the unlikely event that the President's Lady does not take an interest in this aspect, then you most certainly must. I have always born this aspect in mind when making detailed arrangements. It is a sad fact that few people recognise success, but everyone recognises failure. The types of menu card available fall into two main categories. Firstly pictorial cards, which includes the wide range of beautifully decorated cards seen at most functions. The second is the relatively plain card, which we tend to use for chapter functions, printed with maroon text, but the type of card to be used, is of course dependent on normal practice. It is suggested that you obtain a range of sample cards, with the price per 100 cards from a local printer and be careful as there is often a minimum-order quantity. The samples will either be in the form of sample books or loose cards. Printing is a very competitive business, so it is well worth shopping around for the best price.

First Meeting with the President and his Lady

The prime object of this meeting is to explain the responsibilities that fall on the President and to obtain as much information as you can, at this early stage, to reduce the number of times that you have to go back to them saying 'sorry, I forget to mention a few points the other day'. The importance of financial liability has already been stressed and remember to give this aspect the care its importance deserves. As a guide, I have indicated on the main checklist at Appendix 1, whether in my experience the items would normally be paid by the President. All other items, it can be assumed, would be paid from the ticket receipts. As a final reminder, you must ensure that the President is left in no doubt as to what is his financial responsibility and what is not.

Having done your ground work as described in the preparation for this meeting, you should be able to discuss with the President and his Lady and decide on the function date, venue and their requirements for a band, singer or cabaret. It is suggested that you show them a copy of a typical programme for the evening, see Appendix 3 and discuss their role on the evening in very rough outline.

One of the pleasantries for the President and his Lady, during the banquet, is the taking of wine, see the example at Appendix 4. It is important that the taking of wine does not unnecessarily disturb the enjoyment of the meal. The sample taking wine sheet gives a cross section of those selected from the functions that I have arranged. It is suggested that the wine taking be limited to three, after each of the three main courses. It may seem that a maximum of nine wine takings is excessive, but bear in mind that this mainly involves the President and then selected groups of people present. The toastmaster will deal with this aspect on the night, but it is another example of an area where the President and his Lady can tailor this to suit the composition of their party attending the Ladies' Festival. They should be given a copy of the appendix and be asked to give you their requirements. You should explain that although they cannot be considered to be mandatory, it is normal custom and practice to include the first three taking wines on the list. The remaining items are to be at their discretion.

Show the President and his Lady the menu card samples and ask them to make a selection. Make sure that you get a feel for the table colour scheme that they would like and bear in mind that the table clothes, candles and serviettes all come together to form the overall colour scheme for the function. You must ensure that you allow plenty of time to discuss the content of the menu card. The humble menu card contains a great deal of detailed information and must not be dealt with superficially. Refer the President and his Lady again to Appendix 2. It is not my intention to discuss every little item on the menu card format, because some are self explanatory. The front page and first page of the insert, need no input from the President and his Lady. On the second page of the insert, a few examples of suitable quotations are given. You will have noted that many menus do not feature any quotations, but this is clearly an area where the President and his Lady can give some thought, and by looking through books of quotations, stamp their individuality on the occasion. On the third page of the insert, note that the Toast to her Majesty the Queen, is given by the President. The toast to the ladies is given by a brother nominated by the President and his Lady. This brother would normally be a good masonic friend or a relative of the President. It is suggested that the brother proposing the toast to the ladies, also makes the presentation of flowers and the lodge present to the President's Lady. This avoids the situation where brethren are jumping up and down like jack-in-the-boxes. It is suggested that you recommend that a great deal of thought be given to the selection of the person proposing this toast. I once attended a Ladies' Festival where the young brother who proposed the toast to the ladies, spent five minutes telling dubious jokes, while all present sat in embarrassed silence. Amusing anecdotes or stories have there place in mixed company, but I suggest that jokes in poor taste have no place at a Ladies' Festival. The toast to the President is perhaps surprisingly one which many lodges have virtually dispensed with, so it is worth discussing its place in the evening. There is a tendency for this toast to develop into a brother telling those present, what a wonderful person the President is and what a wonderful job he has done in the masonic part of his year. This is often followed by the President confirming, with references to his meetings, that he has had a wonderful year. It is easy for this toast to become a fifteen minute meeting of a masonic mutual admiration society. Do not forget that this is not just a ladies' night, it is a night for the ladies. A significant number of the guests will be ladies plus a number of men who are non masons, who know very little about Freemasonry and this toast can become a crashing bore. In summing up my feelings on this, if your lodge traditionally includes this toast and reply, or the President wants to do it, include it, but ensure that you impress on those involved, to make both elements as light and entertaining as possible and also to keep it short.

If you have used a particular venue before, you may have some sample food menus to show the President and his Lady. If this is not so, it is suggested that you get a feel for their food likes and dislikes, which you will find useful in later discussions with the venue.

Considering the role of the President's Lady. It is important that you be sensitive to her role on the evening of the function. Just think for a moment about what is likely to be required of her. She is going to be the centre of attention for a large part of the evening and would normally be expected to reply to the toast to the ladies. Making the reply to this toast could be a great ordeal for her. It is not everyone who feels happy standing before an audience of 150 guests, or more, to give a speech. Most brethren will have had to stand at meetings or at the festive board to propose or reply to various toasts, but this is not likely to be the case for most ladies, so be sure to discuss this matter with the lady. If the lady is outgoing and full of confidence, then this is not likely to be a problem, but if she is shy, then she may be reluctant. In most cases, with some help and support from the President, she should be able to summon the courage to do the reply herself and if all goes well, as it invariably does, she will be very pleased with herself. You should mention to her that she will have an audience of friends at the banquet, and the whole roomful of people will be willing her to do well. My wife suffered torments on the run up to our Ladies' Festival at the prospect of giving the reply, but was determined to see it through. It is useful to bear in mind that her formula for success was that she insisted on writing her own reply to the toast. She felt strongly, that she would find it difficult to be sincere, when saying someone elses words. Most of us can relate readily to this and she did very well at our Ladies' Festival and I was very proud of her. Facing up to something and beating what you find overpoweringly frightening, calls for real courage. If after discussion it is clear that the lady just cannot manage, you **must** take the pressure off her. There is no point in her making herself ill over what is supposed to be an occasion to remember. The lady may have a daughter or sister who would like to make the reply or there will no doubt be many extrovert friends who will stand in.

We now need to consider the various forms of present, or presentation items. The ladies' present has already been discussed at length, so it is only necessary to clearly lay down the responsibilities for obtaining them. The main questions to be answered are, how many are you going to buy and who is going to buy and/or package them, so note the arrangements on your main checklist. In many lodges the lodge members buy the President's Lady a gift to mark the occasion. The nature of the gift should be for her personally and it is common for the present to be a composite present from the lodge and the President. As a guide, we would normally expect to contribute a sum equivalent to twice the local ticket price, which we would take from the ticket sales and the sum contributed by the President (if any) would of course be solely his business. In my experience, the presentation of the gift to the President's Lady, by the brother proposing the toast to the ladies would normally be referred to as the gift from the lodge. It is also customary, at the same time as the lodge present is given to the President's Lady, that a bouquet of flowers is presented to her. You should also tactfully remind the President that it is also customary for the ladies of the Festival Committee to be presented with a bouquet of flowers. These bouquets would normally be paid for by the President. By the time this first meeting has ended you should have obtained sufficient information to start making detailed arrangements, but beware, there are many factors which can affect the suitability of the choices made by the President and his Lady. For example, do you know positively that their chosen venue has the ability to run your function and will the estimated cost of the function prove to be at a level that will be acceptable to most of the members?

Finance and Ticket Price Calculations

I have already stated the intention to take you through the sequence of arranging Ladies' Festivals chronologically. It may seem strange therefore, in dealing with this aspect before the detailed arrangements have been made. I believe that this is essential because you will need to calculate the function ticket price at a very early stage and also cost must always be at the back of a Festival Secretary's mind at all times. Every arrangement that you make may have financial implications, so don't forget it. The most difficult part of arranging Ladies' Festivals is that they have to be arranged within often very strict financial boundaries. We would all like to be in a position where we could arrange the function of our dreams and just pay the bill at the end of the day. In practice, you will have an income which comes from a ticket price, which you have to match with the outgoings, which are the range of expenses for the function. The start point is often, what price will the guests be prepared to pay to attend the function. There is a considerable amount of work involved in costing the ticket price for functions that you arrange from first principles, because you will normally be responsible for arranging every single detail and if you do not take them all into account, you will find that costs build up and turn what originally looked like a well costed evening into a loss making one. The best advice that I can give on costing the ticket price, is to find out what the attendance would normally be expected to be, for a similar function, then reduce that number by 20-25 per cent. For example, if 125 people would normally attend, cost the ticket price at 100 attending. In my experience you should never deviate from the lower figure. You can almost guarantee that on the one occasion that you say, 'we will be alright with the higher figure', that is when you will have a reduction in the normal attendance and probably risk significant financial loss. Reduced numbers, to those expected, are rarely self adjusting. It can be argued that meals are directly linked to numbers attending and therefore if reduced numbers attend, then this reduces the number of meals that do not have to be paid for, but there are other significant fixed costs, such as the band, toastmaster and possibly some venue costs, which are not. Reduced numbers in this instance means that there are less people to spread the fixed costs over and you have a loss that you cannot make up. It would be unthinkable for the Festival Secretary to have to contact the brethren again, to put out a higher ticket price, so take a great deal of trouble over your estimates from which the ticket price is calculated and make sure that you have considered every possible item of cost. See Appendix 5 as this shows a list of typical items which contribute to the costs of a Ladies' Festival. Notes are also included on calculating the ticket price and in producing the final statement of accounts. If you are 'computer literate', it is an interesting exercise to produce the statement of accounts format on 'spreadsheet' software, where you can vary the fixed and variable costs, to see the effect that this has on the ticket price.

As mentioned, in some instances, the weekend-away functions will effectively be local functions with room booking added to the arrangements. The booking of hotel rooms is potentially a serious source of risk for the Festival Secretary. There is nothing simpler than to book a given number of rooms for the function and hope that all will be well. If you consider that even at heavily discounted rates, it is common for a double hotel room to equate to the cost of a local function ticket. There is nothing wrong in producing a standard format for the brethren, which can be sent to the hotel, but **always** make it clear on the form that the individual bears personal responsibility for his or her hotel booking. Do not forget the example that I gave earlier about the near disaster due to the heavy snowfall. The calculation of the ticket price is exactly the same as in Appendix 5 and you simply include or exclude items as they apply to your function. There is very little to be done in costing for the weekend-away packages which are normally arranged by an agent. You simply obtain details of what is being offered in the package and this is delivered with a range of options, at set costs. The normal options cover the Ladies' Festival banquet and all items associated with it. The length of stay offered under these packages, varies from, full weekend, Saturday and other combinations.

It is also common for additional days stay to be provided off peak at the same favourable terms. An example of the format for a typical weekend package is shown at Appendix 6. You would be wise to check what is being offered in the package, against the checklist at Appendix 1, as what you think is included in the package, is not necessarily what is provided. I suggest that finding out about this on the night of the Ladies' Festival is not going to help anyone. Do not forget that you will still have to go through a simple costing exercise because there could still be some additional items which will affect the ticket price, such as the flowers and lodge present for the President's Lady. The biggest advantage of the complete package, is that all brethren and their guests normally make an approach to the hotel or their agent direct, so that the President and Festival Committee have limited administrative or financial responsibility for the function. This arrangement normally gives very good value for money and a long weekend can be obtained for three times the price of a local function

If the proposed costing procedure mentioned above has been followed, you are likely, on average, to end each function with a small surplus of income over expenditure. You must ensure that when the Ladies' Festival has taken place, that the Festival Treasurer completes a simple statement of accounts, showing income (ticket payments) and expenditure (all costs incurred). You should ensure that the working file that you used for organising the function, is closed with a statement of accounts. I also believe that if the principle of seeing that the matter has been managed well and fairly has been followed, a copy of the statement should also be lodged with the President and the lodge treasurer.

Making Detailed Arrangements

There are, as you will now be aware, many arrangements that have to be made to guarantee a successful Ladies' Festival. There are some items which are fundamental to the running of the function and these must be given absolute priority, because until all of them are made, you cannot assume that your function is going to run. They are, in order of importance, venue, band and to a slightly lesser degree, toastmaster, singer and cabaret. If you remember only one of the key points that I make in this book, I suggest that you note this one. It is perfectly acceptable for you to make any provisional arrangements that you like on the telephone, but **always** follow up in writing and ensure, by referring to your notes on the main checklist, that you get confirmation in writing. Also ensure that you include all relevant detail in your letters of confirmation. There is no point in your meticulously including details of the arrangements with a venue and, then not including the date of the function! I don't think it is necessary to dwell on the common sense of this point, but you could end up with your President and his Lady and a whole roomful of guests, without a band, a toastmaster, or a meal, or any permutation of these. Without written proof that these arrangements have been made, you will have no redress at all. In addition to this, get into the habit of asking every person, or organisation that you approach, to make detailed arrangements, 'are there any other costs that we have not covered?'. I had one bad experience, with a venue, where I had run through all of the items on my checklist, only to find that one month after I had issued the ticket price, the venue mentioned in passing that they make a capitation charge for the function. This meant that the venue made a charge which equated to a 5 per cent increase in cost for each person attending the function. This may not seem very much in isolation, but when multiplied across 150 people attending it became a significant amount, which had not been estimated in the ticket price calculations. Also ensure that when you discuss costs that you confirm the price base that you are working on. There is no point in obtaining costs for a venue, which you will use to calculate the ticket price, if the price is going to change before your function is held. You might be discussing costs a year before the function, so ask if there is going to be a price change before the event? This would clearly play havoc with the costings. Make full use of your main checklist when having discussions with the banqueting staff as I have found that they have always been

THE DUTIES OF THE FESTIVAL SECRETARY

impressed by its use, in that you can run through the arrangements in a business like manner and this has the advantage that you do not waste your time and equally importantly you do not waste theirs. There are other minor arrangements that do not have a significant impact on the evening and these are dealt with later. The main arrangements which need to be made are taken in turn in the recommended order that they should be made. Rather than my keep making reference to the suitability of dates, it is presupposed that your function dates can be met.

Local Venue

You should have obtained sufficient information from the President and his Lady to proceed. You can now make an initial approach to a range of venues and obtain a date which will meet your requirements. It is easiest to do this step on the telephone. Do not at this stage give an indication that you are making a firm booking, because there are many things which you need to check before this can be done. The best way of doing this, is to arrange to meet the banqueting manager. It is important for you to note that the person who makes the detailed arrangement with you, is invariably not present on the night of the function, in that they are office staff, who work 9–5, on Monday to Friday and are not part of the evening banquet team. The first time I discovered this, I was a little concerned. My fears being that something would be lost in the translation between the banqueting manager and the evening staff. My fears proved to be unfounded, in that these staff are very experienced and are arranging functions all day and every day. There are many questions to be asked and detailed requirements to be discussed, so the main points are listed with brief comment:

- Can the venue meet the numbers that you anticipate attending, as your expected numbers may be too high or too low for that venue?

- Discuss the menu, bearing in mind the likes and dislikes of the President and his Lady and obtain copies of the menus on offer, with the prices.

- Obtain details of any alternative main course for vegetarians or for special dietary requirements. In my experience, it is wise to not publicise these alternatives. It is easy to make a rod for your own back as you will find that most people are happy to accept what they are given. If you give a choice you are likely to end up coordinating the allocation of the special meals on the night. Those with genuine requirements will make themselves known in plenty of time in any case. The choice of menu will need to be referred back to the President and his Lady for a decision.

- Obtain a sample wine list, as this is a useful guide to the bar prices and other associated costs. It will also be useful to find out where the wine waiter will be situated for early ordering on the night of the function.

- Are you to be bound by a contract, in which case discuss it and obtain a copy? Ensure that you look at the terms carefully and if possible ask a brother in the lodge who has more relevant experience to check it for you. The bottom line is that you have got to be fully aware of what you are letting yourself in for.

- Are you bound to use a resident band? The band may be excellent, but they may also be very expensive.

- Obtain a sample plan of the function room, with details of the table options available i.e. round or rectangular. Also obtain the numbers that each type of table can seat. Remember that the banqueting manager from experience, knows exactly how many he or she can seat and how to make the room look its best. Also find out how the venue identifies the tables. You will need this for your table-plans. There is little point in your numbering them, when they use lettered table markers, which cannot be changed.

- Arrange for a separate table, adjacent to the top table, for the toastmaster to take his meal and he will use this as his working base.

- Discuss the colour scheme for the table and if possible take along a sample menu card if it is a difficult colour to match. This will include candles, if candelabra are normally provided, serviettes and table clothes. You will find that the banqueting staff will be very co-operative, as it is not in their interest for the hall to be shown at anything but its best.

- Arrange for a microphone to be available in the centre of the President's table. Remember that the toastmaster and President will be used to projecting their voices, but the President's Lady will not. Do not rely on using the band's microphone, it is normally seen as a tool of their trade and will not be available for your use.

- Confirm the split of work between what the banqueting staff are to do on the day of the function and what you will be expected to do. You will find that the function staff normally set out the tables to your plan, they then lay the tables complete with place settings, set the candelabra and the rest will be up to you.

- Obtain the contact name for the day of the function and most importantly, the time that you will be able to gain access to the venue to complete your arrangements. If the banqueting staff cut this too fine, to perhaps reduce the time that they have to pay staff, this will mean that you have to rush to complete your work, so where possible this should be avoided.

- Discuss the location for photographs to be taken and also the area to be used by the President and his Lady when receiving the guests. Again the banqueting staff will no doubt be able to advise.

- Discuss the requirement for band setup time and the options available for band refreshments. Band setup has to be completed in advance of the meal.

- It is important that you ensure that there is adequate car parking. Find out the number of cars that they can cope with and if the venue is new to you, ask if they can provide a map, which you can use when you publicize the function.

- Ask if there are any other costs not discussed?

- Arrange other minor matters, such as tables for raffle prizes and raffle drum, etc.

Use your copy of the main checklist as a reminder for discussions with the banqueting manager and note agreements reached in each area, so that you can confirm at a later date.

Hotel

Some of the main pitfalls in the arrangements made with hotels have already been identified, so it will just be necessary to arrange a meeting to discuss your requirements. If a contract is involved, bear in mind the point made for a local function and check it carefully. The main source of problems, would be if you are asked to contract for minimum numbers attending. Be very careful and only allow yourself to be contracted for what you are sure you can meet. Bear in mind that errors made in this area can be very expensive.

Band

You should already have a feel for the type of band that you require. When you make an approach to a band, do not be afraid to ask questions. Don't loose sight of the fact that you are paying them money to do a job for you. The importance of having a good band cannot be over stressed. We have all been to functions where the band plods through the music, only occasionally being at the right tempo. Big is not necessarily beautiful. Most modern bands are only 3 or 4 piece, but their use of synthesizers and other electronic gadgetry provides a great range of sounds, from what is a relatively small number of instruments. It is preferable to take a band on recommendation, but if this is not possible, ask the band if you can come and see them at another venue. It is easy to overlook some of the fundamental questions which need to be put to the band. What do they charge for a typical Ladies' Festival? This will vary, of course with the length of the evening, but tell them that you want a rough guide. You will need to consider whether you want them to play music over dinner. It is very pleasant listening to music, played at a sensible volume while guests are talking over dinner, but of course this comes at a price. Don't forget to ask them if they can play the 'National Anthem', the 'Ladies' Song', if it applies, 'Masonic Grace' and 'Auld Langs Syne'. It may seem obvious to cover these points, but finding that you are about to sing Masonic Grace at the banquet and the band leader asks 'masonic what'?, is not the time to find this out. The band will need to set up their equipment before the guests arrive and would normally leave a pianist or an organist, to play over dinner. You will need to confirm the band arrival time and make sure this is acceptable to the venue. Be aware that the band cost is very significant when costing the function ticket price, so top bands may be outside your price bracket. For estimating purposes, you will need to consider band food in the interval. You will find that different bands have different expectations in this area and from their own past experiences, you will find that they are not slow to raise the subject and this could be featured in the band contract. If you consider that the band may have left home mid-afternoon on the day of the function and arrive back home in the early hours of the morning. They will have been in an environment where they cannot buy their own food, so I suggest that they have got to be looked after. It may be possible to provide the band members with sandwiches and a drink at the break, but I find this to be somewhat mean. As a routine, I have always arranged for them to be provided with the main course which is to be served at the Ladies' Festival. If you are happy with the information you have obtained, following a provisional booking, you will no doubt be sent a band contract. The information contained in these contracts and terms laid down, are typically, as shown in Appendix 7. As you will see, the contracts are fairly straightforward, but must still be checked through very carefully. They normally include a clause which guarantees them payment to a sliding scale and this is done for very practical reasons. For example, if you cancel the booking 6 months before the agreed performance date, the band stand a chance of obtaining another booking and therefore the cancellation charges are low. If you cancel two weeks before the function, they are unlikely to obtain another booking, in this case the cancellation fee could equate to the full agreed fee.

Toastmaster

In all of the years that I arranged Ladies' Festivals, I was spoiled, in that my dear friend, the late W.Bro. Bill Irons of Rookesley Lodge (No. 8398) was the toastmaster at all my functions and this dramatically reduced any problems that I could have had. When you have confirmed the toastmasters availability, mention that you have organised his table and will ensure that he will be provided with a programme for the evening, a taking wine list and copy of the menu and any other details will be discussed with him on the night of the function. Ensure that you brief him on the start and finish times for the function and outline the scope of his duties, so that he can give you a price for his services. The scope of his work on the evening is important because you may only want him to deal with the early formal part of the evening, then leave the band to perform a 'Master of Ceremonies' role, for the latter part of the evening, or you may require him to go right through to the end of the evening. If the toastmaster suggests that a briefing and programme for the evening are not required. I ask you to bear in mind that before my time in the Festival Secretaries job, we had a toastmaster whose contribution to the early part of the evening was to badly mispronounce the name of our lodge and to announce the wrong name for Madam President, when taking the President and his Lady in to dinner. I suggest that if the professional, who is being paid for his services is not prepared to do his homework, you have got to do some of it for him. The programme for the evening and the taking wine list are dealt with under the next heading.

Singer or Cabaret

It is not necessary to discuss the range of possibilities for this item, because the principles and potential problems are the same as that for making arrangements for a band. I always produce what I call a 'programme for the evening', see an example of this at Appendix 3. This programme gives an outline of the individual items which comprise the Ladies' Festival evening. You will see from this programme that fitting the 'Ladies' Song' into it with an extra song or two, is not a great problem, but a long cabaret, is a different matter. When you make the approach to organise this, ensure that you have a clear idea in your mind as to how long a slot they will be required to fill. This will have some bearing on the price that they charge and will certainly affect whether they can perform at your function as performers may have to co-ordinate the times of performances, so that they can attend other functions, often on the same evening. I have found that most of these performers are very professional and co-operative and the only problem that I have ever had was in getting a cabaret singer to stop once he had started. As you can imagine, this example has an amusing side to it, but short of pushing out a long pole with a hook and dragging him off the stage, there is little that can be done. It can be argued that this act proved to be good value for money, but it had the disadvantage that it dramatically reduced the band-playing time after the interval and this put the evening 'out of balance'. The best way of dealing with this, is to ensure that you discuss the programme for the evening, with clear instructions on the duration of his or her act, with a comment on the undesirability of an overrun.

Printing

You should now be in a position where you can produce a draft of the content of the menu card, complete with all details. As a reminder, the menu card format is shown at Appendix 2. You now have to consider a number of options, all of which can affect the cost of the final printed card. The route that you take, may be driven by financial considerations. It is often a requirement that to make the task cost effective for the printer, you may have to order a minimum quantity of cards, which can be priced by the printer as a complete package, both cards and printing, or if you wish, the cards can be purchased and you then produce the 'inserts' using a word processor. It is a simple matter to use a long reach stapler to attach the insert into the spine of the card. This method has the advantage that you can, to a large degree, control your own destiny. The costs will be reduced, you can reduce the time that it takes to produce the cards and in the unhappy situation that mistakes are made, you can readily make amendments. If you decide to get the printer to do the job, the price will of course increase and it will be necessary for you to co-ordinate the work with the printer. Ensure that you obtain a clear promise for completion of the work. When you have arranged for the printing to be done, I suggest that you **always** ask for a proof copy of the text. The proof copy is just a very rough draft of the text and its intended layout in the menu card. I was faced with a situation where I had arranged my first five functions and had asked the printer for a proof copy every time. On each occasion, I carefully checked the proofs and never found one single mistake. Flushed with confidence, I decided that the proof was unnecessary, so I asked the printer to complete the work straight from the draft. To compound the problem that you may see looming, I had left the collection of the menu cards until the day before the function. To my dismay, the content of the menu card, showed at least fifteen dreadful errors. The printer had taken my handwritten draft and misinterpreted my small 's', which has a tiny loop on the top, as a 'b'. This resulted in 'soup' becoming 'boup' and 'mousse' becoming 'moubbe' and so on. The printer must have had very strange tastes, because I have never come across 'boup' on a menu. The result was that I had to rush round to get the insert reprinted and had to replace the inserts myself. From this incident, another lesson learned, was to ensure that a typed draft menu be sent to the printer, rather than hand written. Just a few words about the printing of entrance tickets. If by custom and practice you have them, or the function is prestigious, then I can see the need for them. In general, I see them as a waste of money, in that they are never called for at the venue and therefore serve no purpose, other than as a reminder of the function date, to those attending. If they are to be produced, the same general points made for arranging the menu card printing apply. The format for the cards can be many and varied, with samples being provided by the printer. The most important aspect is to ensure that all important information is shown on the card. This should include, name and number of the lodge, the words 'Ladies' Festival', the name of the President, the day and full date for the function, the name and address of the venue, the reception time, dinner time, the finish time (often shown as carriages), and the type of dress for the evening (evening dress or lounge suit as appropriate). You will find that there are available, a wide range of novelty items available for Ladies' Festivals, which can be overprinted with the President and his Lady's name, to commemorate the evening, such as book matches, coasters and scarves, etc.

Photographer

Having photographs taken at a Ladies' Festival, can give you a treasured memento of a very enjoyable evening. When an approach is made to a photographer, it would be wise to ask if they have been involved with Ladies' Festivals before. A yes to this question will mean that they will be aware of the normal format for the evening. If they have not, explain that it is a requirement for photographs to be taken at the start of the evening, when the President and his Lady receive their guests. You can explain the arrangements for receiving the guests, but leave the onus on the photographer to make the detailed arrangements with the venue. Confirm the basis on which the photographer operates. Normally, no standing charge is made for their services and they make their money by selling the photographs that they have taken. There should not be any obligation to buy the photographs, which are normally available for viewing later in the evening. Ensure that you confirm the size and cost of the photographs, as you are bound to be asked by someone, in advance, as well as the date and attendance time for the function. The photographer often sends out a form confirming the arrangements that you have made with him. This cannot normally be considered as a contract, but still check it carefully.

Ladies' Presents

Having discussed this subject at length previously, it is not my intention to go into any further detail. The most important point is that you note clearly on your main check-list, who is going to do what and where the responsibility for costs lie.

Ordering flowers

Being perishable items, the bouquets or pot plants, if these are to be used as table prizes, cannot be purchased early, but you need to make some preliminary enquiries and to see where you can obtain the best price. It is worth taking into account whether the function is local or a weekend-away. If local, having the flowers delivered during the day of the function will not normally be a problem, but if it is a weekend-away, how will bouquets stand up to a further day or so in a warm hotel, before the ladies take them home? One solution, is to buy arrangements made of dried flowers, but this must be left to the requirements of the President and his Lady. It is recommended that unless there are strong financial reasons for buying flowers nearer your home, if the function is a weekend-away from home, then buy them from a florist local to the venue, as flowers just do not travel well. It is best to order the flowers a few weeks before the function. There is a considerable amount of work in producing a bouquet and florists will have other work besides yours, so do not think that you can walk into a florist the day before the function and expect them to fall over themselves to meet your modest requirements.

I have found that suitably presented pot plants make excellent table prizes on the night of the function. They improve the appearance of the table and the ladies who win them, always seem pleased to be 'a winner'. The rule of thumb that I use for estimating purposes is to obtain one table prize for every ten people attending. If you find that as you approach the function that attendances are a little higher than expected, then this is an area where you can perhaps spend a little more.

Raffle Tickets and Prizes

We have run a raffle at most of the functions that I have arranged, as it seems to be an opportunity to collect some money for charity, which should not be missed. If this is appropriate, your arrangements must ensure that this must be dealt with as smoothly as possible. I have found that the easiest way of dealing with this, is to place envelopes of raffle tickets in front of the male guests, when setting up on the afternoon of the function and collect the money later. If you decide to take the envelopes round and sell them, then arrange that the raffle ticket seller(s) be ladies. It is amazing how they act as a magnet in drawing the money from the brethrens' pockets. The raffle would normally be dealt with in the interval when the band take a refreshment break and you can also consider asking the President's Lady to assist. Some lodges spend a great deal on raffle prizes. We normally add a sentence to the letter which is sent out informing the brethren of the function, asking 'if they will continue to bring raffle prizes on the night' and we have never been let down. Also bear in mind that you must declare in advance what is to be done with the proceeds of the raffle. If as mentioned previously, the venue cannot provide a raffle drum on the night, you will need to make your own arrangements. The greatest sin when running a raffle, is to run out of tickets on the night. The sight of brethren trying to force money into your hands and you have run out of tickets, is more than a body can bear.

Notifying Brethren of Function Details

You should now be in the position where you have made the bulk of the arrangements and even for the minor items, you should have obtained an estimate of costs, which has enabled you to have decided on a function ticket price. It will be necessary for the Festival Secretary to draft a letter to the members of the lodge, detailing the arrangements that have been made and asking them to make a booking. There is the argument that if you send this letter out too early, it is likely to be forgotten, but the converse of this is, that if you send it out too late, the brethrens diaries will fill up and you may also lose the opportunity of publicising it at lodge of instruction or during a toast at festive boards. On balance, it is recommended that you send out the information as soon as possible. Another useful means of passing out information to the members is via a lodge Newsletter. We have been distributing a Newsletter for some time, with the summons, before each meeting and this is proving to be a very useful vehicle for keeping members in touch with what is happening. An example of a typical letter and booking form are shown at Appendix 8. Separate examples have not been produced for local and weekend-away functions, because the only difference between them, is the reference to hotel bookings. You will find that you will improve the probability of an early response if you inform the brethren that you will take their advance bookings, subject to payment being made by a specific date, nearer the function. If the venue is not well known to the members, it will be very helpful if you can provide a map, which can be sent out with your letter. As an important word of warning. Most Festival Secretaries would normally use their lodge membership list to obtain the names and addresses of members, for distribution of this information. **Please** ensure that you take great care to ensure that you use the latest list and make every effort to ensure that brethren shown on it have not recently passed away. I know of two instances where old lists have been used and widows have had to suffer the upset of receiving Ladies' Festival information, addressed to their husband. It is accepted that these things happen as honest oversights, but we must do everything that we can to minimise the problem. It may be that the President has dual membership of lodges and in this instance, it will be best if you make direct contact with a member of the other lodge. The Festival Secretary of that lodge, if they have one, is a logical choice and he can act as a focus for all detailed arrangements. Some years ago, we held a local function, where failure to take this into account, gave us a problem. On the night of the function, ten guests from the President's other lodge, just did not arrive. You can appreciate that this could have had serious financial implications, as all the meals had to be paid for, apart from the embarrassment of having a gaping hole in the middle of a large table. In this situation the President had acted as the focus for the arrangements, but happily we were able to make contact with another very able brother in the lodge, after the event, who volunteered to deal with the matter for us. The outcome was that eight tickets were later paid for and we did not press for payment for one couple who had a sound compassionate reason for not attending. It is not politic to mention names, but the brother who took this up for us, will be reminded of the occasion when I pass him a signed copy of this book, in gratitude for his kind act.

Dealing with Responses from the Brethren

Obtaining responses from the brethren for Ladies' Festivals, can be one of the most irksome aspects of running Ladies' Festivals. There will be those who come back to you promptly and consider it a point of honour to be first. Then there are the vast majority who will need to be pushed hard up to a few weeks before the function. There is, in my experience, no foolproof remedy. It helps, as mentioned previously, to recognise that people will not part with their money sooner than they have too, so allow them to make advance bookings and pay later. From the first function to the last, I had to resign myself to telephoning those who had not replied, on the run up to the function. Often being greeted with a 'yes of course we are going - we always go'. Under normal circumstances, you will begin to receive at least some completed booking forms from the members. From your meeting with the banqueting manager, you should have obtained a clear picture of the function room layout, table types, numbering system and the number of people that can be seated at each table. Do not make the mistake of launching into the production of a working table plan at an early stage. You will find that the combination of requests to be seated with other parties and natural wastage, will make the drafting of a plan, a total waste of time. I found that the best way of moving towards the production of a table plan, without actually drafting one, was to paperclip the booking forms together into rough table sets for the time being. This has the advantage that although the booking forms are in sets, you can move parties easily from one table set to another if a change has to be made. Do not forget that if you are considering the preparation of a table plan, which for example features round tables with a limit of ten people per table, an increase of only one person in a party can mean that that party will no longer fit onto the nominated table and your plans will be in disarray again. If you find that the table layout recommended by the banqueting manager features a particularly long table, it can be a great help if you divide the table artificially into manageable sections, by marking the divisions using a ribbon or tape and treating the sections, as separate tables for this purpose. If hotel bookings form part of the response, it will help the hotel if you provide them with a separate list of the guests names, complete with their detailed room requirements, taken from the booking forms.

Progressing Arrangements

No hard and fast rules are set down for progressing the work that has been set in motion. The bulk of the actions will fall on yourself and some will no doubt fall on the President and his Lady. It is suggested that you arrange a further meeting with the President and his Lady, some months before the function so that you can run through the detailed arrangements that you have been making. I found that I was continually referring to the main checklist and suggest that you use the copy of this checklist, on which you should have made many manuscript notes, to provide them with an update on your progress. It is very easy for the Festival Secretary to beaver away at his work, and the President and his Lady be left in the dark, wondering what is happening, so avoid this at all cost.

One Month Before the Function

The best suggestion that I can make, when you are dealing with final arrangements, is to complete all actions as soon as you can and not leave them to the last minute. Some items, such as table plans cannot be prepared until all of the booking forms have been received, although some flexibility has to be maintained, because on many occasions I have been changing the table plan up to a day or so before the function. Numbers attending, or not attending at this late stage is a big worry and inevitably you will have to hasten the brethren for the return of the booking forms. I am aware of only one instance, where it looked as though there could be a serious shortfall in attendance, with the possibility that the Ladies' Festival could have been cancelled. If this situation is not managed carefully, by the Festival Secretary, there could be considerable financial loss. It is easy to say that the Festival Secretary cannot force people to attend a function and that is of course true, but there is, in my opinion, a clear course of action to be followed. If the situation is considered in greater depth, the main sin that the Festival Secretary can commit, is to keep the problem to himself. If he does this, the point could be made in a post mortem of the problem that if the brethren of the lodge had been made aware that numbers were dangerously low, then of course they would have rallied round to save the day. The reality is that this may be so, or it may not, but of course this cannot be proven after the event. My suggestion is that, in any situation where you have problems with numbers attending, or rather the lack of them, you must immediately inform the President and then send out a written explanation of the problem to **all** members. You must not pull any punches in this letter, so explain precisely the difficulty that you have; what the financial consequences are and ask for a prompt reply for this call for help. I cannot of course guarantee that this letter will always achieve the desired result, but I can guarantee that no one will be able to point an accusing finger at you for not doing everything in your power to overcome the problem. Also be prepared to have discussion with the venue if you have difficulties. I have always found them to be helpful, particularly if you give them a months notice, rather than telling them a few days before the event. As mentioned previously, I suggested that booking forms are best placed in table sets. When you feel that you have received the bulk of the bookings that you are going to get, it is time to start to prepare a working table plan. If you draw the working table plan as I suggest, it will be your main source of reference, as you run up to the function. The working table plan should be drafted on a sheet, no smaller than about 16 in × 12 in. This is important because you will end up with a large amount of information on this sheet and if produced much smaller, it will be difficult to work with. Use a pencil (so that you can amend) to draw an outline of the function room on this sheet, with the tables drawn to the type and layout as agreed with the banqueting manager. Mark the tables with the identification number or letter agreed with the venue. You now have the skeleton on which you can work. You can now take your table sets of booking sheets and allocate them to a suitable table. I prefer to seat couples adjacent to each other on the same side of the table, rather than seating them opposite each other, as function tables are often very wide and your partner seems to be sitting too far away. It may at first view appear to be unnecessary work, but I have found it best to list the actual names beside each table, again in pencil to cater for the inevitable changes. You will probably find that the name can best be written in the actual seating position for rectangular tables and in a list for each round table. In either instance, if you want certain guests to be facing towards the President's table, simply mark the drawing of the table such that the list of names start at a nominated point and the rest of the names flow clockwise round the table. To illustrate this point, see Appendix 9. You will find that this approach is very useful, because the number of ladies per table, for ladies presents, the placement of place name cards and the placement of table prizes can also be marked. If you have table prizes, it is suggested that you use the time honoured method of choosing winners from the table plan, using a pin. Now and again, I found that lady luck needed a helping hand, to ensure that a newly widowed lady or another deserving case would be guaranteed to win a table prize. Do not bother about trying to keep this plan particularly clean, it is a working plan and will not be seen by those attending the function. You can now produce the place name cards for the table. The place name cards form the basis for setting the table up correctly on the day of the function. These cards can be printed, but I have found that small offcuts of card, folded in half, suit the purpose well. Copy the information from the working table plan going round the table in a clockwise (or the one chosen) direction and produce a place name card for each person attending. Mark the cards as table sets and retain them in sets with an elastic band. You need to be able to assess whether the ladies present can be placed on the table. The size and shape of the present have already been discussed, but it is important to consider the security aspect of these items being on the table in the quiet time between when you set the table up and when the function starts. If this is likely to be a problem, then obtain, a list of table stewards for each table, from the names on the table plan, which you can then pass to the toastmaster on the day of the function. Where possible, ensure that the table stewards are brethren, but in my experience any guest who is given guidance, will be glad to help. Do not forget to nominate raffle ticket sellers, if you are not going to do the job yourself.

Two Weeks Before the Function

You can now complete the draft programme for the evening, as for the example at Appendix 3 and to finalise the taking wine list as for the example at Appendix 4. It would be wise to hold another meeting with the President and his Lady at this time. You should run through your notes on the main checklist and give them a further update on your arrangements, but concentrate on the matters that are going to affect them. They are going to have enough on their mind without worrying about the matters of detail that are your responsibility. Confirm for example, whether the President has purchased the lodge gift for his lady, has he helped his lady to prepare some notes for her reply to the toast to the ladies? Are they happy with the seating of their personal guests on your working table plan? Remind the President that he will have to say a short Grace on arriving at the banqueting table and also suggest that they both give thought to the range of photographs that they would like taken at the function. Consider any other relevant notes that you have made on your main checklist. Before you leave this meeting, make sure that you agree an arrival time on the evening of the function with them. Time is now running out and you must go through the main checklist yourself in much more detail, to confirm that everything has been covered. The venue will no doubt have made clear when they will require final numbers for the banquet and do not forget that you should have arranged a full meal for the toast master and that you have arranged for the band refreshments. It will help the venue a great deal if you pass them a copy of your ever useful working table plan. Remember that the venue normally places the tables in the configuration that you will have agreed with them and they will then set the number of places at each table, as you have indicated on your working table plan. Also ensure that you collect together your requirements for bouquets and pot plants and place your order with the florist. It is now time to consider the preparation of what I shall refer to as the function table plan. On the night of the function, the guests will need a table plan that has just one purpose and that is to enable them to find their table and then find their seating place on that table. The venue normally has a board or easel, outside the function room, on which this table plan can be clipped. Your working table plan will by now be filled with detail and will no doubt have been amended a number of times and have patches of 'liquid paper' all over it. The function table plan must be the opposite of the working table plan, in that it must be presentable, uncluttered and contain only an outline drawing of the tables and their relative place in the function room, with the identification number or letter clearly marked. You will be carrying out the detailed work on the day of the function using your working table plan so for the function table plan, you can simply list the names of those attending, by table and the place name cards will then enable the guests to home-in on their place at table.

A Few Days Before the Function

It is at this stage in the arrangements when I became most apprehensive. Any telephone call could add a few people to a table that was already full, making it necessary for yet more changes to be made to the table plan. It is worth noting that the venue will normally make small changes to the number of meals, this close to the function. It is important to discuss the Festival Secretary's approach to late changes of guest bookings. I have always considered it a point of honour to seat any given party together, however late a change is made. It is not always possible to seat the party with their greater circle of friends, but if it is clear that you have done everything possible to cater for them, most people appreciate that you cannot disrupt the whole room for them. Having checked that all necessary work has been done, your main task is to collect together everything that you need to take to the function, see Appendix 10. If my approach to this part of the planning appears to be over formalised, then consider the problems arising from forgetting to take important items with you to the function. If the function is local, it should not be a problem to drive back home for something, but I suggest that if you are 100 miles from home on a weekend-away, then this is a different matter. I know of one Festival Secretary who forgot to take the menu cards with him and he had to arrange for a brother who was travelling to the function later in the day, to break into his house to collect them for him. My main objective at this time is to do as much work as possible at home, as it is much easier doing this work in comfort, rather than sitting in an empty, cold, function hall. Your planning at this stage should therefore be aimed at allowing you to approach the task of carrying out your part of the setup in the function room, as quickly and as efficiently as possible. Bear in mind that if you are running a local function, you will have to visit the venue, do the necessary work and then go home and change, then get back early to receive the President and his Lady.

Before Leaving for the Function

Collect together all of the items, that are relevant, on your list of things to take with you at Appendix 10 and put them all together in a carton rather than in little piles, which can be overlooked.

During the Day of the Function

One of the first jobs of the day is likely to be to collect or arrange receipt of the flowers, for the President's Lady and the Festival Committee Ladies. If you are using pot plants as table prizes, then these would normally have been purchased from the same source. You may recall that in your meeting with the banqueting manager, you should have obtained a contact at the venue and also confirmed the time that you can gain access to the function room to do your setting up. The first task to perform with the function contact, is to quickly run through the relevant items on the main checklist, to confirm that the arrangements that you made with the banqueting manager have been accurately passed over to the function staff. You may find that the staff at the venue will be a little slow in organising and laying the table to the working table plan that you sent them. It is common for them to forget that you have some work to do after they have finished. I suggest that you arrive a little early and keep an eye on their progress. If things are not moving along as you would wish, a quiet word in the ear of your contact, should move things along. It is best if you wait for the venue staff to complete their work. It is not practical to try to dodge round others who are trying to do their work and in any case it is a formula for error. If you have done the bulk of the work at home, the set up stage will require two or three people. I would recommend that you follow the same set up sequence for any function that you arrange. Your start point will be that tables have been arranged to your table plan, with the place-settings laid. First check that the number of place settings on each table are the same as on your working table plan. If this checks out correctly, take your sets of place name cards, which you have assembled into table-sets and lay them by each place setting, in the sequence that you have marked on your working table plan. It is important that you get a very reliable helper to do this task, as it is pointless in taking a great deal of trouble with a table plan, if the place name settings are not put out in the correct sequence. I always arranged that my wife did this and I then walked round afterwards, doing a quick check of each table. When this has been done, the ladies' places at table can then be identified and menu cards placed in front of each lady. If you have a surplus of menu cards, then some of these can be placed on the President's table, in front of the men as well. You can also place the table prizes in position on the tables, if it proposed to do so, as marked on your table plan. You must also consider whether there are any other novelties or items to be placed on the table, outside those identified in this book. This completes the setting out of the table.

Check that the toastmaster's table has been set up, as it is not appropriate for the toastmaster to sit at the top table. Remember that he has a job to do and in this respect his little table is his office. If he is doing his job properly, he will not have time to engage in small talk for half the evening. Ensure that a menu card, programme for the evening, taking wine list and if necessary a list of table stewards and also a list of table prize winners is placed on the toastmaster's table. As a small plea for toastmasters, remember to ask the President if he will ensure that the wine waiter, or whoever is pouring wine, sees that the toastmaster is provided with a glass of wine during the meal. He will be working and is unlikely to drink very much, but most toastmasters will greatly appreciate this small courtesy.

It will also be wise to ensure that the microphone has been set up at the top table. You will probably find that the venue electrician has had to do this job. Ask to have this facility tested, as it will not help a nervous President or even more nervous President's Lady, if the sound systems squeals from 'feedback' when they try to speak. Also ensure that the President and his Lady are shown how to switch it on and how far they should stand from it when they speak.

If you have not been fully convinced that it is important that you take all of the information that you have produced for the function, such as the file, the booking-forms and the working table plan, then consider the situation that I was confronted with, a number of years ago. The function was a weekend-away and we were only three hours from the start of the banquet. The function table plan was already on display and a guest, unknown to me and happily not a brother, came up to me and said 'my daughter is not shown on the table plan'. Those words are guaranteed, at that stage in the proceedings, to strike fear into the heart. Keeping a clear head, I determined that I would trace the query, in reverse order to the way that the various sources of information had been generated. I double checked the function table plan and the daughter was not listed. That had been produced from the working table plan and she was not on that either. The final source of information was the booking form, which again I had with me and the girl was not on that. At this point, seeing that I was very organised the 'gentleman', rather sheepishly admitted that he had decided that very morning to bring his daughter with him. If I had not had this information with me, I could have been morally obliged to disrupt the table on which they were seated, on the false assumption that I had made a mistake, thereby affecting guests who had taken the trouble to book properly. Despite the circumstances, the gentleman was a little upset that I just could not fit his daughter onto a table that was already full, so I gave him the option of his daughter sitting with his wife and he sitting on the next table for the meal. The moral of this story is that it is a sad fact that some people will use any situation to their own advantage and you being organised and having all sources of information with you, will enable you to deal with the problems. Check that the raffle prize table is in position, if applicable, and that the raffle drum is available. I suggest that you hold back the raffle ticket counterfoils and only put them into the drum just before you draw the raffle. I recall an incident where I had put the counterfoils into the drum, during the afternoon of the function, only to have a member of the venue staff throw them into a skip, believing that they were the old ones from the function the previous evening!

You can also pass the function table plan to your venue contact so that it can be displayed outside the function room.

If the function is local, it will be best if you can go back home and relax for an hour before you start to get ready for the evening. As you will gather, this is going to be a long day. In some respects a weekend-away is easier in that you just have to go up to your room.

The Ladies' Festival Evening

If you have done your planning well, the evening will almost run itself. If you have ensured that the function table plan has been displayed as early as possible, you can rest assured that the guests will check it to see that they have not been missed off. Apart from the incident concerning 'the daughter' that I mentioned earlier, by approaching the exercise methodically, I have never had a single problem. The band should have arrived, in line with the agreed time and the photographer should also have arrived. Ensure that you arrive at the function in plenty of time, in line with that agreed with the President and his Lady. When you have greeted them, it will ease them into the evening if you see that they have a drink and discuss any last minute things that may have arisen. Suggest that the President gives thought to the wine requirements for his table, as you should have arranged for a specific location for the wine waiter to take orders. It is common for the President to be allowed to run a drinks tab, so check that all is well with this. You can run the President and his Lady through the procedure for receiving their guests, where the photographer is to set up for the reception and show them where the microphone is and how it works. Do not worry about this unduly as the toastmaster will look after this. When the toastmaster arrives, you can run through the programme for the evening, the taking-wine list and discuss the other items that you have placed on his table. You should also explain that you would like him to announce the table prize-winners as indicated on the programme. It is not thought necessary to consider every detail of the sequence of events, because the toastmaster will run the evening, but it is felt that there is some merit in amplifying a few important points by running through the sequence for the evening using the programme for the evening that you have produced, based on Appendix 3. The following comments are made in the same order as this appendix, but the sub headings have been amalgamated where appropriate.

Presentation of Guests

This should be one of the most enjoyable parts of the evening. The President and his Lady, have the opportunity to be congratulated by their friends and members of the lodge. The President and his Lady will receive their guests at the place agreed at the meeting with the venue. The toastmaster will introduce the guests by name and they will be greeted by the President and his Lady. As Festival Secretary, be sensitive to the time that this phase is taking and if necessary give the toastmaster some quiet assistance in ensuring that the guests move promptly from the bar to be presented to the President and his Lady.

Photographs

The onus is clearly on the President and his Lady to ensure that they have sufficient photographs taken and hopefully as you should have pre-warned them, that this should be dealt with fairly quickly. The photographer will undoubtedly be co-operative, as taking a dozen photographs of couples or family groups could significantly increase his sale of photographs later in the evening.

Escorting President and Lady to the table – President say Grace

The toastmaster will lead the couple to their place at table. The President must be ready to say Grace on reaching the table. The sequence is that the toastmaster will gavel and the President will then say Grace.

Taking Wine During the Meal

It is not intended to go into much detail on this aspect, as a sample Taking Wine List is shown at Appendix 4. To minimise the disruption to the meal, the taking of wine will normally be after each course. You will note, that when the President's table has finished the first course, other tables will be part way through their first course, but this cannot be helped. The toastmaster will take the lead and announce each taking of wine. There is a minor but important piece of etiquette here. Brief the President and his Lady to sweep their glass from one side of the room to the other when taking wine. It is irritating as a guest, to have got to your feet, to see the President and his Lady raising their glasses to the few tables directly in front of them and appearing to ignore half of the room, on either side.

Masonic Grace

When coffee has been served, the toastmaster will say 'pray silence for Grace which will be sung'. The toastmaster should have arranged a signal with the band leader, if they are not familiar with the procedure. Bear in mind that the brethren of the lodge are often outnumbered by non-masons at Ladies' Festivals, so the toastmaster should draw attention to the fact that the words of the Grace are printed inside the menu card.

The Loyal Toast

There is often confusion over the sequence of events at this stage. Again the toastmaster must have informed the band of the correct sequence, if they are not familiar with the procedure. My old friend, W.Bro. Bill Irons, used to give me a string of words which helped me to remember the sequence and they are, SAY, SIP AND SIT. Expanded, this gives the sequence:

SAY   The toastmaster will say, 'will you kindly rise for the Loyal Toast to be given by the President. The President then says 'The Queen'.

SING   The National Anthem will then be sung.

SIP   All raise glasses.

SIT   All present do just that.

Distribution of Ladies' Presents

You should have provided the toastmaster with the names of brethren who are to act as table stewards, which you obtained from the working table plan. It is not a problem if you have overlooked this. Ask the toastmaster to request that a brother from each table act as table steward, ensuring that they count the number of ladies on their table, before they come up to see the Festival Secretary. I believe that in a world which lacks a little, old world charm, it adds to the evening if the table stewards collect a reward for distributing the presents in the form of a kiss on the cheek. If you have done this job properly, you will have nominated table stewards and you will know exactly how many ladies are on each table, from the working table plan. To further simplify the process, you could consider putting the correct number of presents into a bag for each table steward.

Toast to the Ladies and the Reply

As suggested earlier, it is recommended that the brother who proposes the Toast to the Ladies, should for convenience, be the same brother who makes the presentation of the lodge gift and the flowers to the President's Lady. It is all too easy for the brother proposing the toast, to end up with armfuls of speaking notes, the present and a bouquet of flowers. It is suggested that the sequence be:

> The toastmaster will say 'I claim attention to W.Bro............, who will propose the toast to the Ladies and also make the presentation of the lodge gift and flowers to the President's Lady'.

The relevant brother will then propose the Toast to the Ladies.

The brother then makes the presentation to the President's Lady, who will pass the present on to someone close to hand.

The brother can then present the President's Lady with the flowers, which can also be passed on.

The toastmaster will then say 'I claim attention to Madam President for a reply'.

The lady will then deliver her speech of reply.

Comment has been made earlier about the difficulty for the President's Lady in making this reply. At best, the Lady will be nervous and at worst, she will be terrified. The toastmaster will control the situation, but all present must stay quiet and morally give the lady as much support as possible. I suggest that it will be plain bad manners if even mild heckling occurs, as the average lady, will just not be able to deal with this.

Toast to the President and the Reply (if applicable)

It is not my intention to go into any more detail on this aspect, other than to say that the toastmaster will announce both the brother who is to propose the toast and the President when he makes a reply.

Drawing of Table Prize-Winners

The toastmaster will simply have to read out the prize-winners for each table, using the information that you have provided earlier. Try to ensure that when the table prize-winners are announced, that the prize is presented to the lady winner, by a brother on her table. This is a suitable time for your raffle ticket-sellers to pass round the room.

Presentation to the Festival Committee

The President will no doubt wish to say a few words of thanks to the Festival Committee, so to prevent the committee members being stranded

THE DUTIES OF THE FESTIVAL SECRETARY

somewhere between their table and the position in front of the President's table, it will be best if the toastmaster says 'I claim attention to the President who will say some words of thanks and will then call the Festival Committee and their ladies to his table, so that he can make a presentation'. In any case, just be sensitive to the way this pans out.

President and his Lady retire

This closes the first part of the Ladies' Festival and completes the formalities for the evening. The practice of retiring from the banqueting room can serve a number of purposes. The first very practical point is that if there is not a separate room for dancing, then the banqueting staff will need the time to rearrange the tables, to give sufficient space for dancing. Normally the guests will retain the same tables, but ensure that the President and his party are looked after. The second reason for retiring is to enable the President and his Lady to withdraw from the limelight that they will have been in for some time and enable them to relax for a short time in the bar, with their family and friends.

Let Dancing Begin

The toastmaster will co-ordinate the start of dancing with the band leader. It is normal custom for the President and his Lady to start the dancing. The toastmaster should be sensitive to whether the President and his Lady are happy with this. If they are not particularly confident, he can announce that 'the President and his Lady have requested that you join them'. The guests can then enjoy this informal phase of the evening. The only problem that I have found with this part of the evening, is that of the music being played too loud. If you have done your research well, you should have booked the type of band that will suit the majority of your lodge members, but never all of them of course. As Festival Secretary, you can rest assured that you will be told if there is a problem. You will have to be the supreme diplomat over this issue. If you get the odd complaint, then stand in the room and try to make an objective assessment yourself. If you feel that the complaint is unjustified, then do your best to ignore the complaint, bearing in mind that against the one complaint, you could have a hundred people who are having a glorious time. If you start to get a number of complains, then speak to the band leader. I had one instance where the band leader reduced the volume for five minutes, then increased the volume again. There is a tendency for some musicians to play the music for their own gratification. In these situations, I have no hesitation in reminding the band leader who is paying for his services for the evening and payment is dependent on a performance that is satisfactory, in all respects.

Interval for a Band Break

The toastmaster will again liaise with the band leader to decide on the timing for this and you should have arranged for band refreshments. Ensure that you extend the courtesies to the band. In all probability they will have worked hard and apart from the food that will have been provided, take them into the bar and buy them a drink. If you have arranged a cabaret, then this must be timed for this period. If you have not, the time can usefully be taken up in drawing the raffle. You should have arranged for a raffle drum or a suitable substitute and the prizes should be in place on a table where the guests can see them. If you have arranged for the President's Lady to assist in drawing the winning tickets, she can assist the toastmaster, or any other brother who is conducting the draw. Have a suitable brother at the raffle table to assist in issuing the prizes. When the winners start to come up to collect their prizes, do your best to see that ladies are escorted. There is a growing tendency for 'gentlemen' to allow their lady to collect the prize on there own. To some ladies, the prospect of having to cross an open dance floor, perhaps on high heels, with every eye appearing to be focused on them, can be a little daunting, so brethren, let us be sensitive to this situation and do our best to see that others follow the same code. The Festival Secretary must be alive to the length of the band break. It must not be excessive, and must certainly not be allowed to leave a dull patch in the proceedings. Once dancing has recommenced, you can then take a break yourself and enjoy the dancing.

Closing of the Festival

The toastmaster should ensure that the evening will end at the time agreed with the banqueting manager. Depending on lodge custom, the evening often ends with a circle being formed and the singing of 'Auld Lang Syne'. If this is the custom, the President and his Lady would stand in the centre of the circle, during this song. When this has ended, if it is the custom to 'chair' the President, ensure that you have earmarked two fit members of the Lodge, of similar stature, to perform this task. At the same time, arrange for a strong Brother to walk round behind the chairing party to assist, should it be necessary, as you will clearly not want to end an enjoyable evening by injuring the President. After this, the toastmaster should announce that the President would like to say a few words. This will normally take the form of thanking everybody for attending the function, thanking the toastmaster for his good works and also thanking the band. The evening will no doubt end with the President wishing those present, a safe journey home, or a safe trip to their room, if the venue is a hotel.

After Formal Closure of the Evening

The guests will probably remain in the hall for a short time, discussing the evening with their friends, but your responsibilities to the guests will not be over until you have seen that the President and his Lady, or other guests, are happy and have no problems. You will now have other important matters to deal with. Most importantly, you must register with the banqueting representative, any problems with the arrangements for the evening, particularly where there may be a dispute over payment. If a problem of this nature arises, ensure that you register it clearly and make a note to put this in writing as soon as possible. If the complaint is not self evident, for example, it concerns poor food, insufficient food, or cold food, obtain witnesses, before you leave the venue, in case there is a failure to agree. Most venues will be very reasonable over complains, as they will not wish to cause bad feeling and thus prevent the possibility of your return on a future occasion, so don't be too shy. It will now be necessary for you, or the Festival Treasurer to pay the toastmaster, band, singer or cabaret. You should have checked when the arrangements were made, how this should be done. If you have arranged a drinks tab for the President, this would normally be payed by him before he leaves the function. I have known agreement to be reached, whereby he is billed after the event. There is the danger that you get into a 'its all over mode', so think carefully about items which you will need to take away with you. Most venues run functions similar to your own, night after night and anything left behind is likely to disappear without trace. You will need to collect your own papers, there may be spare ladies presents, so it is good practice to take a slow walk around the hall for items which guests may have left behind, for example.

The Week Following the Function

The Festival Treasurer can now take stock of the financial aspects of the function. Hopefully your estimates will have been accurate and the safe costing figure used for your ticket price calculations will have ensured that you are in a sound financial condition. It will be necessary for you to arrange the transfer of funds to charity from the proceeds of the raffle. Considering the sums of money involved, business cash flow means that the bill from the venue, normally for the meals and any venue cost that may apply, will be sent to you without delay. If you have a Festival Treasurer, he should check the bill very carefully with you before payment is made. As mentioned, take prompt action to resolve any problems with the venue, in writing and/or revisiting the venue can also save a great deal of time in 'correspondence tennis'. When all costs have been collected, you should be in a position where you can produce a simple statement of accounts, as shown at Appendix 5. I have already discussed the importance of this aspect and feel strongly that to show complete openness of your dealings, the Festival Treasurer or yourself, as applicable, should send a copy of this statement to the President and the Treasurer of the lodge. Also ensure that you close your job file with a copy of the statement of accounts, in deference to its importance. I believe that it is also important to retain all papers relating to the function, particularly those that have financial implications, so that at any time questions can be answered. It has not been practice in my lodge to carry out an audit function on the arrangements, but if by custom and practice this is required to be done, then so be it. Do not forget the point made earlier in this book, that you will have been managing other peoples money and full visibility of information should be made. To support this point, I have retained the files for every function that I have arranged, and as you can imagine, they have proved to be invaluable as reference for this book.

Lessons learned

If you are a new Festival Secretary and this is your first function, you will no doubt have learned a great deal. It is important that you do no waste the knowledge that you have gained. As mentioned at the start of this book, there is no merit in keep making the same silly mistakes. It is very unlikely that your function will be identical to the examples that I have given, so you should reflect on the effectiveness of your arrangements. Did the band and the toastmaster come up to your expectations and did your arrangements prove to be as effective when implemented as you had expected? If you are to avoid making the same mistakes over again, you have got to take some positive action. In my masonic and business life I have found that any important action taken should be considered as a 'closed loop'. After the function you can consider the effectiveness of the arrangements. If they have worked well, then no action needs to be taken.

If they have not, then corrective action needs to be taken and your checklists can be amended, ready for the next function. I can guarantee that if you continually use this approach, your checklists will improve progressively, until in the end, they will reflect your requirements exactly and each successive function will run like clockwork. An added bonus is that the information that you have produced will prove to be invaluable when, as will inevitably happen, you have to help another brother to take over the Festival Secretaries' duties, when you move on to other masonic work.

Closing Remarks

I enjoyed my 6 years as Festival Secretary very much and I hope I have convinced those not previously involved in arranging formal functions that it involves far more work than is appreciated by most brethren. To plan, arrange and conduct a Ladies' Festival, to budget and without problems, is reward in itself, but to also receive the warm thanks from the President and his Lady, can be considered to be the icing on the cake. An added bonus is that you will find that a closeness develops between the President, his lady and yourself, which will stay with you for the years to come. I hope also that I have convinced you that my approach to the task is not unduly pedantic, or if it is, that there are good reasons for it being so. I once had a psychological profile conducted on me, in conjunction with my work. I was found to be a coordinator and an implementer. Having got to know me a little throughout this book, you can perhaps be the best judge of the accuracy of the profile. I hope with all my heart that you have enjoyed this book and have learned enough to take the fears away from arranging these functions and that this will encourage you to take the job on yourself, if you have not already done so.

Appendix 1

Main Ladies'
Festival Checklist

Very Important Notes

Enter brief notes of all arrangements made, on your version of Appendix 1 and check progress regularly.

It is assumed that you have confirmed that the function date and time can be met,

Make provisional bookings by telephone.

Always confirm bookings in writing.

Note on a copy of this checklist, who is going to be responsible for **every** item.

Venue

Book function date, 12-18 months in advance, or as soon as possible and consider implications of winter dates.

Ensure venue can accept your likely numbers attending, minimum and maximum.

Agree function times (send programme for the evening later, see Appendix 3).

Check terms of contract – **carefully**.

Ask for **all** associated costs.

Ask for a map to the venue, if it is not familiar to members.

Obtain detail of table shape and size options

How are tables normally laid out in hall.

Find out table letter or numbering system.

Find out where the President is normally presented to the guests.

Confirm where the President's top table would normally be.

Find out where the photographer would normally work.

Find out where the function table plan would be placed (board or easel)

Ask if they have a raffle drum (if required)

Ask the venue to provide a raffle prizes table (if required).

Do they provide candelabra for the tables.

Confirm venue provide and agree on serviette colours to match menu cards and candles.

Arrange for a microphone for the top table and drawing raffle.

Arrange for the toastmasters table and find out where this is normally put.

What time can you gain access to the venue, on the day of the function, to 'set out'.

Ask about the security of things that you leave on the afternoon, such as ladies' presents, etc.

Any other limitations or restrictions.

Obtaining an evening contact name – will not be banqueting manager.

Find out final date to submit numbers attending function.

Arrange for brethren to chair President at end of evening, plus a safety man.

Hotel

Do they offer an all in weekend package. See Appendix 6.

If not, ensure that responsibilities are clearly agreed.

Tell them that the Festival Committee will be responsible for the function and the lodge members are to pay their own hotel bills.

Obtain options available on length of stay and prices.

Any single or special children's rates and are dogs allowed.

Meal

Obtain range of menus, with prices **that apply to the date of your function**.

Enquire if it is possible to mix and match items on the menu.

Check on the possibility of vegetarian, or special diet meals.

President and lady select – careful, this is a major cost.

Agree number of meals at the appropriate time – don't forget band meals and toastmaster.

Bar/Wine

Obtain sample wine list and price list, **that apply to the date of your function.**

Find out where wine can be booked on the evening (wine table normally)

Get a feel for drink prices.

Arrange to run a drinks tab for the President's table, if he wants it (President pays for).

Car Parking

Where is the car park.

Where is the access to it.

What capacity does it have.

Any overspill arrangements.

Band

See example of a band contract at Appendix 7 and check **carefully** when received.

Select band by recommendation if possible and bear in mind, this is a major cost.

Obtain band business cards when you or friends attend other Ladies' Festivals.

What type of music do you want.

Agree arrival, set up, start and finish times.

What is the fee for the times required.

What do you get for your money (how many band members).

Will they be required to play dinner music.

Can they play, 'Masonic Grace', the 'Ladies' Song', the 'National Anthem' and 'Old Langs Syne'.

What do they expect regarding drink and food for the band break.

At the appropriate time, give them an outline of the programme for the evening, at Appendix 3.

Singer/Cabaret (President pays for)

Agree performance times – to link up with your programme.

What do you get for your money.

Agree their fee.

Control them – overrunning the programme gives problems.

Toastmaster

Ensure you get agreement on the scope of his work.

Agree his fee.

Ensure he is fully briefed, see programme for the evening at Appendix 3.

Prepare him a taking wine list, see Appendix 4.

Ensure he is given a menu card.

Prepare him a list of table prize winners.

Prepare him a list of ladies-present table stewards.

See that he gets a glass of wine during the meal.

Photographer

They do not normally make a standing charge, but check.

Agree a start time and give them a contact name at the venue – they make detailed arrangements with venue.

Ask for the size and cost per photo.

Get a guide to when and where the prints will be available at the venue.

Menu Cards

See sample menu card at Appendix 2.

Cards are placed in front of each lady and if sufficient, place more on the top table.

Obtain samples or selection books from printer.

Obtain prices, with printing.

Confirm minimum order quantity (common for this to be 100 cards).

Check time from ordering to completion of work (leave plenty of time).

Do you want to buy the cards and print the inserts yourself.

Put to Madam President to choose – consider as part of table colour scheme.

Draft contents (typed not manuscript) and check **carefully**.

Order the cards.

Ask for a proof copy and check **carefully** – never dispense with a proof copy.

Collect cards in good time and carefully check a good sample quantity.

Entrance Tickets

Unless it is your custom or function is prestigious, we do not bother with, but if you do, follow the principles, as for the menu cards.

Raffle

Mention at the festive boards and in your letter of invitation that raffle prizes would be appreciated.

Buy tickets – have plenty.

Arrange for a raffle drum with venue.

Arrange a prize table with the venue.

Sell envelopes, not tickets, to save time.

Arrange for your raffle ticket sellers.

Squash counterfoils – don't fold them – it saves time in drawing them.

Ask President's Lady (in advance) to assist on the night, when drawing the tickets.

Decide where proceeds are to go when post-function costing is completed.

Main Ladies present

Allow for the fact that on average, 55 per cent of those attending will be ladies.

Check on the last five years' presents to avoid duplication.

Consider obtaining from trade sources, lodge contacts or specialist suppliers.

If possible get sale or return.

Check prices for the present and any packaging.

Confirm availability and delivery.

Consider size of present – will it clutter the table, or will you need table stewards.

Consider security problems, if leaving presents at the venue in the afternoon.

Minor Ladies Present

If the income from attendance is higher than estimated, consider giving each lady another small present, such as a scarf, fan, flower in her glass, etc., but only late in the day when you are sure of attendance.

Novelty items

Obtain items such as personalised book matches, coasters or scarves, etc.

Table Prizes

It is common for this to be a pot plant.

Obtain costs and estimate on one table prize every ten people attending.

Use a pin or any method to select a lady prize winner from the working table plan.

Give the names of the winners to the toastmaster, so he can announce.

Watch costs, they soon mount up.

Place-Name Cards

These can be purpose bought or off-cuts of card can be used.

Produce them from the working table plan.

Check them **carefully**.

Elastic band them into table sets.

Ensure on the night that you have spare cards and liquid paper, in case of problems.

Flowers for Madam President

Normally a spray, but may have to be different if the venue is a hotel and the flowers cannot be kept.

Any special requirements, such as an orchid, or posy (President pays).

Lodge Gift To President's Lady

The Festival Secretary donates a sum, on behalf of the lodge, that is approximately twice a local ticket price (from the ticket price).

Indicate to the President that he may add to it himself.

This is traditionally still referred to as the present from the lodge.

You should have already confirmed who will make the presentation, when drafting the menu – normally the brother proposing the Toast to the Ladies.

Gift To The Festival Committee (President pays)

It is necessary, to save the President embarrassment, to inform him that it is normal for him to buy flowers or a little gift for the wives of the Festival Committee.

Combined letter notifying of function and Booking Form

An example of this format is shown at Appendix 8.

List of items to be taken to the function

Due to its importance, it is well worth checking through the list of things to take to the function at Appendix 10.

Finance

Ladies' Festival estimating and statement of accounts are detailed at Appendix 5.

Register any significant problems with the venue staff on the evening of the function and confirm in writing.

The Festival Treasurer needs to consider the methods of payment for:

Venue/meals – normally invoice after function.

Hotel bookings – **ensure individuals are responsible**.

Band – prefer cash.

Toastmaster – prefers cash.

Singer/cabaret – prefer cash.

President's wine and drink tab – can normally arrange for him to pay by cheque at the end of the evening.

Produce statement of accounts, see Appendix 5.

Appendix 2

Layout of Typical Menu Card

There are many variations in layout for the menu card, so the following information is a composite of those seen and includes a few ideas for the addition of some quotations as personal touches. It will improve the appearance of the menu if all text is centred on the page by the printer, as is the content of the menu items, shown below.

Front Page of Menu Card

The amount of text that can be put on this page is often dictated by the design on the front of the pictorial card, but should contain at least the following information. If there is no room on the front of the card for overprinting, some or all of this information can be placed on the first page inside the card and other pages moved back one place. This leads to some duplication of information, but there is plenty of room because the insert is normally made by folding an A4 size page in half and this gives four page faces of A5 size:

Lodge name and number

𝕷𝖆𝖉𝖎𝖊𝖘' 𝕱𝖊𝖘𝖙𝖎𝖛𝖆𝖑

President:

W.Bro...

Day, full date of function

First Page of Insert

The insert is the set of printed pages, which are stapled into the inside of the menu card. If an insert is not used, be guided by the printer who will have far more experience than you in this matter:

Name of Province/District/Area

Graphic of lodge crest [if required]

Lodge name and number

𝕷𝖆𝖉𝖎𝖊𝖘' 𝕱𝖊𝖘𝖙𝖎𝖛𝖆𝖑

President:

W.Bro..

Day, full date of function

Name of venue and town

Second page of Insert

You can insert suitable words of welcome and good wishes for a happy evening, with a suitable quotation to follow – '*Wine to drink and food to eat, but best of all, good friends to meet.*'

Detail the items on the menu, down the page as follows:

Course 1

❁❁❁

Course 2

❁❁❁

Course 3, etc.

❁❁❁

Suitable quotation:

'*Serenely full, the epicure would say, fate cannot harm me, I have dined today.*'

GRACE

From the 'Laudi Spirituali' A.D. 1545
For these and all Thy mercies given,
We bless and praise Thy name O Lord.
May we receive them with thanksgiving,
Ever trusting in Thy Word.
To Thee alone be honour, glory
Now and henceforth for evermore.

Amen

Third page of Insert

Toasts

Useful quotations:

'I don't care how much a man talks, if he says it in a few words.'
John Billings

or

'Life is short, why should speeches be long'

HER MAJESTY THE QUEEN

Proposed by

.... (The President)

THE LADIES

Proposed by

W.Bro./Bro. ....

W.Bro. ....

will make a presentation to the President's Lady

Response by

.... (President's Lady)

THE PRESIDENT

Proposed by

W.Bro./Bro. ....

Response by

.... (The President)

67

Fourth page of Insert

Entertainment

Music during dinner by

.... (name)

Music for dancing by

.... (name of band)

Useful quotation:
'There followed a display of dancing, the likes of which had never been seen.'

or

'Show me the fox that ever trotted thus.'

Singer or Cabaret [name if applicable]

Toastmaster

.... (masonic rank and name as applicable)

Festival Secretary/Committee

.... (masonic ranks and names)

Useful quotation:
'Good Night Sweet Ladies, Good Night'
Hamlet

If the above information fits onto three pages, it is useful to bear in mind that the fourth page can be headed 'Autographs' and becomes a useful keepsake for the function. I have also seen a menu where the space was used by including a section called the 'Birds' Eye View'. This section contained quotations from the ladies of lodge members, to whom they were attributed by name and some examples are given as follows:

'I can get him to speak alright, but who's going to get him to stop.'

'Whenever there's something I want him to do, he's always off to a Committee Meeting.'

'His friends aren't the fair weather kind – they always come here when they're in trouble.'

'I don't mind him not being able to dance, but I wish he'd stop trying.'

Appendix 3

A Typical Programme

Reception .... (example 6.00pm for 6.30pm)

Dinner at.. (example 7.00pm)

Carriages .... (example 1.00am)

Example of Programme for the Evening: (day) (full date)

Lodge Name:.. (**Important** Followed by a phonetic pronunciation for the toastmaster if necessary).

President : W/Bro..

Madam President :....................(Christian Name or that by which she would like to be announced by the toastmaster and surname if different to the President).

Presentation of all guests to President and Lady (give location at venue).

Photographs to be taken (give location).

Toastmaster escorts President and his Lady to their table.

President to say Grace (on reaching the table).

Commence dinner, taking wine between courses (see Taking Wine List at Appendix 4).

When coffee is served – toastmaster says – 'pray silence for Grace, which will be sung' (Words are shown on the menu card, see Appendix 2.)

Start the formal toasts: toastmaster announces 'the Loyal Toast. The Queen (National Anthem).'

Table stewards to report to Festival Secretary to collect ladies' presents or if not arranged, ask toastmaster to call for a brother from each table.

Toast to the ladies – announce singer (if applicable) – toastmaster says 'I claim attention to W.Bro/Bro.......... who will also make the presentation of the lodge gift and flowers to the President's Lady.'

Toastmaster says 'I claim attention to Madam President for a reply.'

Toast to the President – the Toastmaster says 'I claim attention to W.Bro............., our President (if included).'

Claim attention to the President for a reply (if included).

Toastmaster draw tickets for table prizes and Festival Committee sell raffle tickets.

Claim attention to President, who will call up Festival Committee and Lady(s), to thank them and make a presentation.

Toastmaster announces that the President and Lady are to retire.

Let dancing begin – President and his Lady lead the dancing.

Band break – announce cabaret – draw raffle – President's Lady to assist?

Close the evening – form a circle for 'Auld Lang Syne' – chair the President.

Final words from the President .

Appendix 4

Example of
Taking Wine List

The following is only a guide to the type of the taking wines that can be carried out on the evening. The President may have a large family and will wish to extend this aspect. You would normally be expected to include the first three items shown and you should try to have no more than three taking wines after each of the three main courses, during the banquet.

After the first course of the meal

1. The President with all the ladies.

2. Madam President with all the gentlemen (they will stand).

3. The President with his own dear lady.

After the second course of the meal

4. The President and his Lady with their family and equally importantly, their partners.

5. The President and his Lady with their invited guests.

6. The President and his Lady with members of (lodge name) lodge and their ladies.

EXAMPLE OF TAKING WINE LIST

After the third course of the meal

7. The President and his Lady with members of all other lodges and their ladies.

8. The President and his Lady with anyone who has a birthday today.

9. The President and his Lady with all non-masons and their ladies – and in doing so, he thanks you for your support.

10. The President and his Lady with the Festival Committee.

The toastmaster takes the lead in announcing these items.

Appendix 5

Ladies'
Festival Costing

Elements of cost

It is first necessary for you to appreciate the individual elements of cost which build up to the total cost of the function. The following items are a cross section taken from the functions that I have arranged to date, so you can consider those that apply to your specific function:

Venue costs:
   Venue fee (if any)
   Staff gratuities on the evening of the function.
Cost of meals for menu chosen.
Costs related to band:
   Band fee
   Cost of band food and drinks
Toastmasters fee.
Singers fee.
Cabaret fee.
Menu cards and cost of printing.
Invitation cards and cost of printing.
Ladies' presents:
   Cost of presents
   Packaging costs (if any)

President's Lady:
> Presentation flowers.
> Contribution to the gift from the lodge.

Table prizes purchased.
Raffle prizes purchased.
Novelty items purchased.
Stamps and stationary.
Ticket refunds (if any).
Any donations made to the evening by brethren.

Important

Remember that you must estimate for all costs, however small, so double check that you have listed those costs that relate to the function that you are arranging.

Calculation of Ticket Price

The calculation of the function ticket price is best explained using the format for the final statement of accounts. This is in principle a very simple format which shows the Income, which is normally the receipts in the form of the ticket price that you had set for the function plus other items, as shown below and the expenditure is the list of items, similar to those elements of cost above. The following gives a guide to the layout of a statement of accounts, on which the calculation of ticket price will be explained.

INCOME		£ TOTAL
'x' attending @ 'y' £ per ticket.	=	....
Proceeds from raffle.	=	....
Any donations made to the evening by brethren.	=	....
Income sub total	=	_____

EXPENDITURE

Venue fee (normally fixed cost).   = ... *

Staff gratuities on the evening (fixed cost).   = ...

Meals – 'x' meals @ .... £ per head.   = ... *

Band fee (fixed cost).   = ... *

Band food and drinks (fixed cost).   = ... *

Toastmasters fee (fixed cost).   = ... *

Singer's fee (fixed cost).   = ... *

Cabaret fee (fixed cost).   = ... *

Menu cards and cost of printing (fixed cost).   = ... *

Invitation cards and cost of printing (fixed cost).   = ... *

Ladies present – 'z' presents @ ...... £ per present. = ... *

Ladies present packaging costs (fixed cost).   = ... *

Novelty items.   = ... *

President's Lady –

   presentation flowers (fixed cost). = ... *

President's Lady – gift from the lodge (fixed cost). = ... *

Cost of table prizes.   = ... *

Cost of raffle prizes (fixed cost).   = ... *

Stamps, stationary and photocopying (fixed cost).   = ...

Ticket refunds (if any).   = ...

Expenditure sub total   =   _____

The balance will be INCOME minus
EXPENDITURE.   =   _____

There is nothing difficult in calculating the ticket price. Just deal with the matter methodically and you will not have any problems. Look at the information shown under the statement of accounts above. You will see that only the meals for the Ladies' Festival and the ladies present, vary with the number attending the function and the rest of the costs are fixed. A star (*) has been marked beside all of the items under EXPENDITURE which can be accurately predicted at a very early stage in the arrangements.

It is suggested that you start with a blank copy of the statement of accounts format. If at the earliest stage in your arrangements, you fill in the information that is 'dotted' under the EXPENDITURE sub heading, it can be seen that the bulk of the information that is required for this sub total will already have been obtained. If not, these estimated costs can be obtained by asking the venue, band and toastmaster, etc., for budget costs to enable you to calculate the ticket price. This information will be gladly given by those concerned. Be sure to obtain the prices that will apply for the date of your function, which could be a year away, If these adjustments are not available, varying the costs in line with inflation will normally suffice. The last piece of information that has to be inserted in your format is the number attending the function marked 'x'. Do not forget, as explained in the text of the book, to insert a safe attendance figure when calculating the ticket price. The costs in the EXPENDITURE column can then be added to give an expenditure sub total and this is then divided by the safe number attending and you have your ticket price, shown at position 'y' under the INCOME sub heading. The few items that are not marked with a star (*) are relatively minor, such as the postage and gratuities, etc. When considering postage bear in mind that it will be necessary for you to send out the notification of the function to all members and if you double this cost, in most cases this will meet the other unspecified postage costs. It cannot be stressed too highly that great care must be taken at this stage, as any problems that result from poor estimating could be very large ones.

Statement of Accounts

You should produce a statement of accounts when the function is completed and all actual costs are known. If the balance is negative, ie. the expenditure was higher than your income, then the function clearly ran at a loss. Hopefully, you will have given your estimate of the ticket price, the consideration it deserves and the balance will be positive. It would normally be expected that the proceeds of the raffle would be donated to charity, but any other surplus should be clearly entered as a surplus and be retained for deposits or other payments that have to be made at an early stage. I have found that a surplus of about eight times a local ticket price is essential to cater for deposits, or any item that has to be paid, before the income, in the form of ticket receipts, for any given function is to hand. The statement of accounts is produced, simply by inserting actual figures in the above format when the job is completed. It will be a useful exercise to compare your original estimates, that you used for the ticket price calculation, with the actual costs and note where you need to tighten up your estimating for future functions. Remember, if you have done something wrong, amend your checklists, so that you do not make the same mistake again.

Appendix 6

Example of a Typical Weekend-Away Package

There are a wide variety of weekend-away ladies festivals, so the following should be considered to be a representative example of the type of information that would be provided by the venue:

General information provided:

Description and address of the hotel.
Description of the room and its facilities.
List of leisure facilities.
Prices (£):
> Full weekend............
> Saturday night only............
> Banquet only............
> Extra days stay............
> Special prices for children and single guests............

Programme for the weekend, with timings:

Friday

3.00pm onwards.	Arrival and welcome.
7.00pm – 8.30pm.	Dinner and coffee.
8.30pm – 12.00pm.	Cold supper for late arrivals.
9.00pm – 12.00pm.	Dancing.

Saturday

8.30am – 9.45am.	Full English breakfast.
1.00pm – 2.00pm.	Bar lunches available (not inclusive)
5.45pm – 6.20pm.	Reception by the President and his Lady. (photographer in attendance).
6.30pm – 8.30pm.	Seven course musical banquet.
8.30pm – 9.15pm.	Draw for the table prizes. Distribution of ladies' presents. The Toasts.
10.00pm – 1.00am.	Dancing.
11.15pm – 11.45pm.	The cabaret.

Sunday

8.30am – 9.45am.	Full English breakfast.
1.00pm – 2.00pm.	Luncheon, coffee and departure.

Appendix 7

Example of a
Band Contract

You will find that band contracts will vary, but the following example can be considered to be representative and does clearly illustrate the point, that the longer you leave cancellation of the band, the more it will cost you:

Band name, address and the contact telephone number of band leader......................

Clients name, address and telephone number..................(the Festival Secretary)

Dear........... (name of Festival Secretary)

I have pleasure in confirming your booking of .... (band name) to appear as follows:

DATE ....(of function)

VENUE ....(name and address)

TYPE OF FUNCTION ....(name of lodge and ladies festival)

PLAYING TIMES................(example – 9.15pm to 12.00pm)

SET UP BY.......... (example 7.00pm)

ARRIVAL TIME...........(example – one hour prior to set up time)

BAND FEE £.......... (may be a note to indicate payment is required in cash)

SPECIAL ARRANGEMENTS
>   Taped music through dinner........(ticked if applicable)
>   Live music through dinner (extra fee)............(ticked if applicable)
>   Hot meal for 4 piece band...............(ticked)
>   Other..............

CANCELLATION CHARGES
Any cancellation of this booking will render the client (the Festival Secretary) subject to a cancellation fee as follows:
>   On contract..........(example – 10 per cent of full fee)
>   Within 28 days of function date...........(example – 50 per cent of full fee)
>   Within 7 days of the function date............(example – full fee)

The above details constitute a binding agreement.

PLEASE SIGN AND RETURN THE DUPLICATE COPY TO THE ABOVE ADDRESS WITHIN 14 DAYS TO CONFIRM THIS BOOKING.

We look forward to a successful and enjoyable function.

Signed for..(the band name).   Dated..............

Signed by the client.....................(the Festival Secretary).   Dated..............

Appendix 8

Example of a Combined Letter Notifying Brethren of the Function and Booking Form

---

The example shown below, is suitable for a local function, or a weekend away, as the only difference between them, is the reference to hotel bookings, which can be included or excluded , as appropriate:

LODGE NAME AND NUMBER

Festival Secretary's Address.
Tel Number.
Fax Number.
(Date)

Ladies' Festival (Year)

...........................(Names of President and his Lady) Ladies' Festival is to be held at the.................. (Name and address of the venue) on ....(Full date). The reception will be at ....(time) and dinner will be served at............ (time). Carriages will be at.......... (time).

Dress is formal.

The Ladies' Festival ticket price is £........

Accommodation: (Specify hotel room options available and give costs). As usual, accommodation bills are to be settled personally with the hotel. Will you please note that there will/could (include as appropriate) be charges for accommodation or dining on a sliding scale, up to the date of the function, if any cancellation is made.

Specify further details, as provided by the venue, if the function is a package weekend away. (As shown in the example at Appendix 6).

The usual raffle will be run and we hope that the generous donation of raffle prizes will continue. (You **must** say which charity is going to benefit from the proceeds at this stage.)

Will you please fill in the booking form below and return it to me as soon as possible. In view of the contract that we have had to sign, guaranteeing minimum numbers for dining and accommodation, we must have a clear indication of numbers attending by.......... (date), when the sliding scale of costs start to take effect.

Booking forms are more important than cheques, so please help us reduce the big telephone ring round.

...................................(Festival Secretary's signature block)
Festival Secretary

FUNCTION BOOKING FORM
(Lodge Name and Number)
(Venue)
(Date of function)

Surname	Initials	Masonic Rank/ Mr/Mrs, etc.	Hotel Booking Requirements (Indicate Single or Double)	Names of Parties to be Seated with you

(Continued as necessary)

Cheque Number.............   Name of lodge member...............(Print)

.... (Signed)

Date........................

If the letter introducing the function is short, this booking sheet can be included at the bottom of the letter, as a tear off slip, but if this is not possible, issue a separate sheet. Allow space for approximately 10 names, as this will meet most requirements.

Appendix 9

Sequence for entering names on working table plan

Rectangular Table

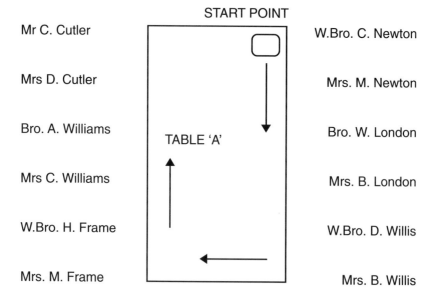

Mr C. Cutler	START POINT	W.Bro. C. Newton
Mrs D. Cutler		Mrs. M. Newton
Bro. A. Williams	TABLE 'A'	Bro. W. London
Mrs C. Williams		Mrs. B. London
W.Bro. H. Frame		W.Bro. D. Willis
Mrs. M. Frame		Mrs. B. Willis

Round Table

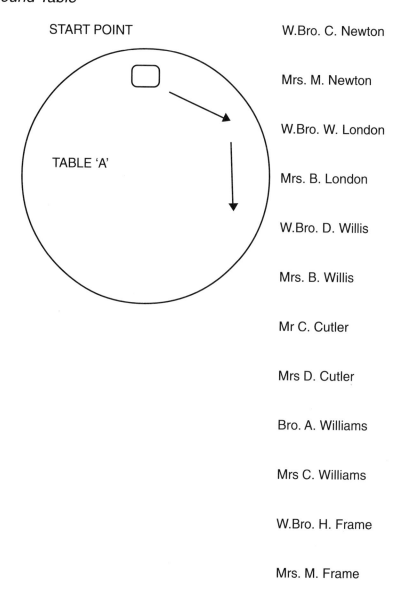

START POINT

TABLE 'A'

W.Bro. C. Newton

Mrs. M. Newton

W.Bro. W. London

Mrs. B. London

W.Bro. D. Willis

Mrs. B. Willis

Mr C. Cutler

Mrs D. Cutler

Bro. A. Williams

Mrs C. Williams

W.Bro. H. Frame

Mrs. M. Frame

Appendix 10

List of Things to take to the Function

This list has been prepared from the items that have ever appeared on my check lists. You must ensure that you check through your version of the main checklist at Appendix 1, to see whether you have added other items. It is also useful to add a column to the right hand side of the page, indicating who is responsible for seeing that the items gets to the function, if you are not doing everything yourself. If applicable, ensure that you send those responsible, a copy of the completed checklist as a reminder of the actions that they are to take.

Required on arrival at the venue

Your main checklist, with any notes you may have made, for discussion with function staff.

Function table plan, with a few drawing-pins, or any sticky fixer that will not damage the surface of the display board.

Setting up the table

Working table plan

Sets of place name cards, including spares and a pen.

Menu cards, including spares.

Table prizes.

Serviettes – venue normally provides.

Any other minor items, such as book matches, or any other table novelty.

Setting up the raffle

Tickets or envelopes.
Prizes.
Ticket counterfoils.
Raffle drum, or substitute

Required for the evening

Programme for the evening (copy for President, toastmaster and brother proposing toast).
Taking wine list (copy for President and toastmaster).
Any spare copies of speaking notes for the President, or his Lady.
List of table prize winners (copy for toastmaster)
List of table stewards to distribute the ladies present.
Lodge gift for the President's Lady.
Ladies' presents, including spares.
List of ladies' presents, by table, if required.
Flowers:
    Lodge to the President's Lady.
    From the President to the Festival Committee ladies.
    Any special requirement, such as a posy or orchid.

For use of the Festival Secretary, in the event of problems

Ladies' Festival file, with all correspondence.
Booking forms, in table sets.
Accommodation details, if the function is at a hotel.

Financial

Your draft estimates, based on the statement of accounts at Appendix 5.
Means of payment for band, toastmaster, cabaret, (likely to be cash).

Cheques which have to be passed to the Festival Treasurer.

Have enough cash for your own use.

I hope it is clear that due to the potential number of items involved, you should resist the temptation to either rely solely on your memory, or use the 'throw it all in the car at the last minute' technique.